PRAISE FOR **SUSTAINABLE**

Not since Og Mandino's **THE GREATEST SALESMAN IN THE WORLD,** *has an author packed so much wisdom into so few pages. Whether you are a manufacturer, retailer or service provider, this entertaining book gives owners the road map to build better businesses, more durable families and inspiring lives. Refreshingly original, poignant and impactful,* **SUSTAINABLE** *is a fictional gem from the pen of an author who has clearly lived what he has written.*

Tom Deans, Ph.D., author of
EVERY FAMILY'S BUSINESS AND WILLING WISDOM

I've known Josh for several years. Over that time, he's present-ed at several Book Yourself Solid meetings. He always has ideas that are practical and can be used in both small and large businesses. He's helped me think about my business in different ways and this book will help you think about your business in a different way as well. Read it. You'll be glad you did.

Michael Port, best-selling author of
BOOK YOURSELF SOLID and **STEAL THE SHOW**
and co-founder of **HEROIC PUBLIC SPEAKING**

I've known Josh for over fifteen years. I've learned that Josh is one of the few advisors in the private business world who un-derstands what drives value in a private business. You would do well to read this book and apply its message.

Rob Slee, author of **TIME REALLY IS MONEY**

Josh Patrick knows how to unstick your business and help it become economically—and personally—sustainable. In a world awash with buzzwords and business fads, it's refreshing to find an entertaining story that brims with real-world application. **SUSTAINABLE** *will take you on a journey to discover the five keys to unlocking the untapped potential in your enterprise.*

Steve Farber, author of **THE RADICAL LEAP**,
THE RADICAL EDGE, and **GREATER THAN YOURSELF**

This is not your normal business book. Much of it reads like a novel, with real people and real problems, presented as they occur in the real world. At the core, it's about staying simple and focusing on what really matters, a collection of practical lessons that apply to anybody who is seriously trying to run and grow a business. **SUSTAINABLE** *is the core, and the book will help you achieve that.*

Tim Berry, founder of **PALO ALTO SOFTWARE** and
well-known business blogger

Sustainable:

A Fable About Creating a Personally and Economically Sustainable Business

Josh Patrick

Disclaimer:

This publication is designed to provide information about the subject matter covered. It is sold with the understanding that neither the author nor the publisher is engaged by the reader to render legal, financial, investment, accounting or other professional service or advice. The purpose of this book is to educate and entertain. Neither the author nor the publisher, Summit Press Publishing, shall have any liability or responsibility to any person or entity with respect to any loss or damage caused, or alleged to be caused, directly or indirectly by the information contained in this book.

ISBN-13: 978-1979981620

For more information, visit *www.sustainablebusiness.co*

Published by

Summit Press Publishing
Green Cove Springs, Fl
phone 860-306-4057
fax 860-281-2750
www.summit-success.com

Cover and interior design by S. Peter Lewis

*To my father, Ben Patrick,
my first mentor who taught me that business
is about doing the right thing: providing a
great product with honesty.*

TABLE OF **CONTENTS**

Introduction..13

Chapter 1: John's Dilemma...16

Chapter 2: Help's On The Way...23

Chapter 3: Change Is Hard... 27

Chapter 4: Values Matter... 34

Chapter 5: Walking The Truth... 42

Chapter 6: The Objective Review Continues... 48

Chapter 7:The Venerable Mission Statement...................55

Chapter 8: The Core Value Analysis... 61

Chapter 9: Big Rocks And The $5,000 Per Hour Job... 78

Chapter 10: Dinner For Three... 86

Chapter 11: The Breakfast Of Champions......................101

Chapter 12: Operational Irrelevance Is The Goal.............112

Chapter 13: The Effects Of Financial Insecurity... 120

Chapter 14: Financial Challenges Arrive... 124

Chapter 15: Living With The Mission Statement..............134

Chapter 16: Identifying The Best Customer.....................140

Chapter 17: Alignment Across The Board.........................153

Chapter 18: Tying Up Loose Ends... 158

Recommended Reading List... 168

Cool Stuff... 176

Acknowledgments... 177

About The Author... 179

INTRODUCTION

I first met Josh at a writer's retreat Michael Port and I were hosting. I tried to pour several margaritas down his throat but, much to my chagrin, I found out he was a red wine person and there wasn't any convincing him of the errors of his ways.

Over the past year or so, I've had the opportunity to appear on Josh's podcast and I've had him on my podcast. Between the writer's retreat and the other opportunities I've had to talk with Josh, I've found that he is dialed into what it takes for a business to last past the current owners of the business.

And, that's exactly what this book is about: what it takes for a business to become economically and personally sustainable. You'll take a trip into the life of the Aardvark family where you might find some similarities that exist in your business.

You'll learn what the five areas of sustainability are and you'll pick up some tools and tricks that will allow you to start thinking about your business in a different manner. One of these is near and dear to my heart. That's putting together a business that makes enough money for it to be sustainable.

In my book, *Profit First,* I talk about using different bank accounts for different uses. For example, you want one account for profit, one for taxes, one for living expenses and one for operational expenses. One of the five areas of sustainability is making enough money. Josh told me that my account system provided him the idea that a business should have four areas of profitability to become sustainable.

I won't tell you the four areas, you'll just have to read the book. And, I do hope you will read the book. It'll help

you look at your business in a different way. After you read *Sustainable*, you'll see your business in a different light. You'll look at your business and find out that if you can't get yourself out of the way, you'll never be able to successfully transfer your business.

Too often I see business writers and consultants take something that is, at its core, simple and make it way too complicated. Josh has simplified the process of what you need to do to create a sustainable business and he's done it in a fun way through the eyes of a frustrated business owner. I want you to read this book and then read *Profit First* by none other than me. The combination will start you down the road of owning a business you'll be glad to own and you'll be even more happy when it's time to move on to what's next in your life.

Mike Michalowicz, author of *Profit First*,
The Pumpkin Plan, *The Toilet Paper Entrepreneur*,
and *Surge*

CHAPTER 1: **JOHN'S DILEMMA**

John Aardvark has lots of problems. Aardvark Manufacturing, the company he founded and owns, is stuck and about to go into a major crisis. For the third time in less than two months, Aardvark Manufacturing has been late on a delivery to their largest client, XY Medical.

John and his wife, Anne, are having their morning coffee, talking about their upcoming vacation. Anne has been asking John to take a vacation and he has been putting her off until now. It's never been easy for him to find the time.

Just as they finish their coffee, just as John gets up from the table to head to work, the phone rings. John always cringes when the phone rings. Too often it means that something is going seriously wrong. This time is no different.

John picks up the phone. His wife looks at him. No doubt his facial expression has changed. It always does. No doubt she's thinking to herself that he had better not be considering cancelling their vacation. Because he is. John has already cancelled a scheduled vacation three other times over the past two years, always at the last minute.

"I don't care what you have to do. Just get that shipment out the door," John finally shouts. "And it better not have any defects."

Anne gives John a sour look. She would know from his tone that he's talking to their son, Adam. These days, all John does is yell at Adam.

John continues with his voice all but busting a hole in the ceiling. "Adam, you are just a total waste of time. Why is it that I've got to save your bacon almost every day? I'm getting really sick of this. You and I are going to have a serious talk when I get into the office."

John slams down the phone.

"What does this mean about our vacation?" Anne asks.

John scowls at her. "I have no idea. I've got to get to the plant right now. XY is about to pull their entire order from us. If I don't fix it, and I'm the only who can right now, we're going to lose 40% of our business. If we lose their business, I'm not sure how the company is going to stay afloat. And another thing, don't even think about defending that no-good son of yours. He's the reason we're in this pickle."

As soon as John starts talking about their son, Anne loses her temper. "John, why do you always blame Adam?"

John is no longer listening. He grabs his bag and heads for the door.

"And I hope you don't think that you're going to cancel our vacation," Anne yells after him. "What's the point of having your own company if you can't take time off? We haven't had a real vacation in five years. Taking a long weekend a couple times a year does nothing for you. And it certainly doesn't do anything for us."

"You're just being unreasonable. We'll take a vacation just as soon as I get the company back in control. I can't leave now because we have a big customer that's ready to walk and I'm the only one who can fix the problem."

Anne snorts and stalks out of the room, but not before taking a parting shot. "If you were smart, you wouldn't have these problems. Maybe you should take a good look in the mirror. You're not the only one who can fix this. I'm really sick of you thinking you're the only one who has any talent at your company."

John stands in the middle of the living room. Once Anne slams the door behind her, he slumps down onto the sectional sofa. *Anne doesn't understand the problems and pressures I'm under*, he thinks, *I wish she would understand that I can't just pick up and leave any time I want.*

He doesn't have time to sulk. Even he knows this. He puts on his coat and storms out the door, slamming it behind

him. Not an unusual way for him to be starting his day; hasn't been for the past two years.

In his gut, John knows the sources of his problem even if he can't quite put his finger on why or when they started spelling trouble for his company. One of them is Stan Socket, the sales guy, or at least he thinks Stan's the problem.

Stan is what you would expect to see in a guy who's been selling for 30 years. He comes from the school where salespeople are supposed to sell, and more closes means better sales. Unfortunately, Stan has been left behind. What works today is not even close to what worked when Stan started selling. For the first 20 years, Stan was a very successful salesperson. Then his sales started to stagnate. John is having a hard time getting Stan motivated to make the calls he should.

Stan has been with Aardvark Manufacturing for 25 years. He joined the company before there were computers or contract-relations management systems, when Aardvark's competition was limited and mostly domestic. Back then selling was relatively simple and easy. Much has changed. Now Aardvark Manufacturing's competition includes Asian, German and French companies, and the competition has the latest technology and systems in place to compete with Aardvark. Stan's still doing things the way they were done in the 1980s.

The first person John sees when he walks into the plant is Stan. He pulls Stan into his office and starts to bully him. "Stan, do you know that XY is about to cancel all of their contracts with us? How come I needed to find this out first thing in the morning from that good-for-nothing son of my mine? Aren't you supposed to be on top of what's going on with our clients? You know that XY is our biggest customer and if we lose them it's going to be your fault. If they walk, I don't even know if our company can survive."

Stan stares at John like a deer in the headlights. John is tired of that look because all employees give it to him when he takes them to task.

Stan hesitates, as if to offer a response. But he chooses otherwise. Everyone knows that when John starts one of his screaming rants, it's just best to let the storm pass and continue with the task at hand. And that's exactly what Stan does.

All these things would spell trouble even if John recognized them for what they are, but he doesn't. He has only a vague, mostly subconscious sense about what's wrong. And this makes the situation worse.

John turns his attention back to Stan. "Stan, don't you have anything to say for yourself?"

Stan takes a step back, as if forced into a corner. He hesitates for a moment. "John, don't you remember I told you that XY called me two weeks ago and told us that if we had any more quality problems they were going to start looking for another supplier? I don't think this is something I can help with now. If we're going to save this account, I think you're going to have to call them yourself."

John scowls. "Just get out of here. I see that I have to solve this like always. First, I have to go back to shipping, find that no-good son of mine and find out what we need to do to get our shipment to XY today. I'll deal with you later."

Stan slinks out the door. He turns to look at John over his shoulder, as if wondering whether this is the time John will actually fire him.

All this might come as a surprise to outsiders. At a glance, Aardvark Manufacturing would seem a sophisticated operation. The plant looks like a modern, state-of-the-art facility. Like many privately held companies, however, things on the outside look much better than they are on the inside.

John doesn't realize the problems he causes. He thinks everything at Aardvark is someone else's fault. He thinks that if only his people would step up everything would be great.

John is a control freak. Not being very self-aware, he doesn't really think about this. But because his management style is very hands-on, and because there are no systems in place, he's at the center of all decisions, large and small. He believes this enables his company to provide better service.

John doesn't know it but he needs help. If he continues down this road, the outcomes he wants for himself, his family and his company will never be met. In fact, there's a very good chance, as John is about to discover, that he's not ever going to be able to retire, something that he's sure to find disturbing.

John thinks about the most recent fight he had with Anne that morning as he storms out of his office into the plant entrance. He replays it like a scratched record in his head.

"I don't understand why you can't take time off. All our neighbors take time off."

"All our neighbors have jobs working for other companies. They don't work for themselves. They don't have a business to run."

He thinks of the way his wife's face turned red, the way her voice rose.

The pressures of owning and running a family business are nothing new to John. He's felt them for years and can trace some of the problems he's having now to always trying to please others rather than doing what he feels is best.

John is totally frustrated. He doesn't know in what direction to turn. He spends all his time putting out fires and has no time to think about strategies for his business. He's ready to throw in the towel. He's feeling about as low as he's ever felt. He feels like a failure and doesn't know where to begin to turn things around.

Just as he's wondering what to do about Anne, he walks into the finishing department where he finds Adam under a new machine, the very one that was supposed to be working properly months before. Clearly, it's still not operational. Adam has told John that the reason shipments are late is because this machine keeps breaking and they don't seem to know how to fix it.

John walks up to Adam with a little too much energy. "Adam, what are you doing under that machine and why haven't you told me that the XY shipment that was promised for last week hasn't gone out the door yet?"

Adam climbs out from under the machine. "What do you expect me to do? I told you this machine was a piece of junk, but all you do is yell at me and tell me to get it working. Why haven't you called the manufacturer and gotten a mechanic from the company to come in and fix it?"

John's face glows red. "What's your problem? You never told me we needed to get someone from the factory here. You keep telling me that we've almost got this machine working right, and here it is keeping a shipment from going out to our best customer. Here's what I want you to do. I want you to move this shipment away from this machine, go to our old machine, and get this shipment out the door today, and I don't want any excuses."

With that John storms out the door and goes back to his office. He slumps into his chair, puts his head in his hands, and wonders what he's going to do. He knows he can't keep going like this.

At one point, business was fun, not anymore. He knows that if he doesn't take care of his problems, there's a good chance his business will evaporate, and he's not quite sure where to turn.

The one thing he knows is that he needs to call their contact at XY and see what he can do to save the account. Maybe

if he gives them a big discount, he'll be able to get them to give Aardvark one last chance.

XY has threatened to pull the plug before. This time it feels different and in John's gut he knows this may be the very last chance he has with XY. The problem is John really doesn't have a good idea about where to turn or what to do next. He's sure of one thing, there's no way he can share his worries with anyone else in the company, not even Anne.

All is not lost. Even though this feels like the worst day of his life, John will meet someone who can help him with his dilemma. John has been lucky with his business. When things look the bleakest, there's always something that comes along to keep him from the brink. He certainly hopes the same will hold true this time. But will it?

CHAPTER 2: **HELP'S ON THE WAY**

John has had a tough day. Not only has he had tough conversations with his wife, his son, and his salesperson, he has to go to a chamber social event, the last thing he wants to do.

When he arrives at the event, he makes a beeline for the bar. There he runs into one of the few people he thinks could possibly help with his problem, his lawyer, Jim Langley. He knows his lawyer had some problems with his firm years ago and, since then, things seem to have gone well for him. Thinking he has nothing to lose, John approaches Jim, takes a big swig of his drink, and says hello.

Jim takes one look at John, whom he's known for almost as long as John's been in business, and says, "You look terrible. What's up?"

John tells him about his day. He talks about his conversation with Anne, his son, and how he's about to lose his biggest account. In total frustration, he asks, "Do you think it's time for me to sell? Or do you have any better ideas?"

John's lawyer looks away. His forehead wrinkles in thought. He hesitates before he speaks, but then he says, "John, it sounds like you need some serious help. Talk to this guy, Aaron, who sometimes goes by the name, The Curmudgeon." Jim takes a sip of his own drink. "But I do have to warn you. If you're not going to be serious about fixing your company, don't bother. Aaron is a no-nonsense guy and isn't going to put up with anyone who isn't serious about making their business sustainable."

John gives his lawyer a dismissive wave. "Why in the world would I want to talk to him?" he says. "I hate consultants. They never bring any value to the table. And what's

this stuff about sustainable? I have little interest in taking on extra expenses right now. I just can't afford it."

Not only does John not like delegating authority, but also he's never been inclined to ask anyone for a hand. He's only hired a consultant a couple of times in the years he's owned his business. And although he's had outside advisors before, he's generally been unhappy with the advice they've offered. They've come up with lots of ideas but have done little to help implement them beyond leaving John 300-page reports that he has no time to read. With only 15 minutes here or 15 minutes there to devote to anything extra, John shelves long reports and ends up never using them, much less reading them.

But he has to do something. He's up against the wall with his son's counterproductive behavior, the prospect of losing a major client and his wife's demands to take a vacation. He needs help and he knows it.

The relationship between the two men is old and strong, which is likely why Jim ignores John's protest. "Not sustainable in an environmental way, although that might not be a bad idea. When Aaron says sustainable, he means making your business economically and personally viable, continuous, and long-lasting. That's what got me to say yes to the idea of working with him. It was the first time a consultant started talking about things I was interested in."

John pauses to consider the lawyer's recommendation. Jim appears confident, relaxed, happy. He's a different man, now that his business is thriving. Even John can see that.

"This guy has a different way of working on things," Jim continues. "He doesn't view himself as a consultant. He doesn't view himself as a coach. He sort of views himself as a mentor. But mostly he sees himself as a thinking partner, someone whose job is to help you come to terms with things you already know. When I hired him, I was stuck. Like you, I was ready to pull the plug. Then Aaron came in asked me

a bunch of great questions, and before long, I started down the long road back. He helped me remember what I already knew or should have known. That's what he does. At the end of the day, he doesn't believe he's going to tell you anything you don't already know. But he'll be there to help you think through those things in ways you probably haven't considered before."

"Sounds reasonable. At the same time, I wonder why I need to hire someone who is going to tell me things I already know."

Jim spreads his palms open, as if acknowledging the obvious dilemma. Yet, John is not doing well. He's admitted as much to himself and to his friend.

"I'm tired of dealing with presumptuous consultants who think they know all sorts of things about my business that I don't," John says, unwilling to cede the argument. Then he remembers the problems back at the plant, with his wife at home. Jim raises an eyebrow and takes yet another sip of his drink. "But having someone come in and help me think through my problems in ways that make sense to me has to be better than getting some wordy report handed down from on high. What did you say he calls himself? Kerr Mudgen? Is that M-U-D-G-E-N?"

The lawyer stifles a laugh. "It's not Kerr Mudgen; it's Curmudgeon," he says.

"Curmudgeon? Why do you call him that?"

"That's what he calls himself. But after you get to know him, you'll probably just end up calling him by his real name, Aaron. I will say, there were times when I hated working with him. He made me ask myself questions I never had considered before, and he made me look in the mirror till I figured out most of my problems. I'd caused most of them, and most of them I could fix."

John falls silent for a moment. Could this Aaron really help turn the ship around?

"My law firm was falling apart. We were losing money. We lost a couple of good attorneys, too, and it looked like a few more were getting ready to walk out the door. I had to do something and, like you, I was at the end of my rope. I even thought about chucking the whole firm and giving up both the law and my law practice."

"That certainly is where I'm at."

Jim takes a drink and continues. "He helped me turn my firm around. Now, I love to go to work, and lawyers are dying to work with us. It's a great place to be." He writes the phone number on the back of a napkin and hands it to John. "Call him. The conversation won't cost you anything, and you might even learn a thing or two about your situation."

John considers the napkin. Heck, worst case scenario, he can use it to wipe up the mess he has on his hands.

Jim glances over John's shoulder and waves at another client. He excuses himself, leaving John to his own thoughts.

I might as well give him a call, John thinks. He looks at the phone number. *Tomorrow.* He lets out a sigh. John knows it's time to work on his problems and he wonders if this Aaron guy, who thinks he's a curmudgeon, can help. The worst that can happen; it'll be a wasted phone call.

CHAPTER 3: **CHANGE IS HARD**

The next day, John is dragging. He's tired. He had another fight with his wife about taking a vacation, and he knows he has to deal with his best customer. He also knows that if he doesn't do something, there's a good chance he will blow his marriage and his business.

John picks up the phone, hesitates, and puts it back down on the base.

He picks it up again, takes a deep breath, and punches in the Curmudgeon's number.

"This is John Aardvark and my lawyer said I should talk to you. He said you'd be expecting my call." John squeezes the bridge of his nose. "I'm not really quite sure how you're going to help me, but I've got some issues with my business, and my lawyer told me you could help."

Aaron was expecting the call. He's had many calls start the same way. Sometimes the person on the other end of the line thinks the world has come to an end. Other times, the caller sounds like John, annoyed that he even has to make the call, skeptical.

"If it's any consolation, John, a lot of business owners don't know what they should be doing. And many of them don't even know that they don't know. That you do know you have problems suggests you're at least headed in the right direction."

John likes the sound of the Curmudgeon's voice. Because much of what he does is gut driven, John decides to invite him to his office for a discussion. He really doesn't have anything to lose, he thinks and, who knows, he might even learn something that could be useful.

Early the next morning, the two men meet in John's office. The sun is low and bright in the east-facing window behind John's desk, so they opt for easy chairs in the corner by the door, where Aaron won't have to squint against the light.

John's office isn't especially fancy, but it looks thoroughly lived in. Pictures of his family hang on the walls which make the comfortable seating area they move toward that much more inviting. John prefers sitting in the seating area instead of behind his desk. He wonders whether this is the right thing to be doing now. He doesn't want to let Aaron get the upper hand. John feels out of control and doesn't want this consultant to know it. John thinks he's open, but the truth is he's not the most trusting person and letting Aaron know how he's really feeling would put him at a disadvantage.

Taking a seat, John sizes up his guest. Aaron is bald except for thin, graying hair on the sides of his head. The consultant has on a dark sport coat over a crisp, blue, button-down shirt, open at the collar. His eyes, framed by no-nonsense rectangular black-framed glasses, are friendly but they're so penetrating they make John uncomfortable.

"John," Aaron says, "this is how we're going to start today's conversation. We're going to spend an hour, maybe an hour and a half, conducting what I call the Alignment Conversation. The conversation has four parts. They're all based on what would make your life better. First, we want to understand where you are now; second, we want to find out where you would like to be in three to five years; third, we want to really understand what the difference is between the two; and finally, we want to know what the personal and economic value is in solving the issues you identify."

John listens closely as Aaron continues.

"Why don't we start with where you are now? We covered much of that in our phone conversation yesterday. You mentioned your late shipments to your best customer, your son

being a problem both at work and at home, your wife being angry about not taking vacations, and the feeling that your sales process is really out of date."

Nodding, John confirms the lay of the land. *At least Aaron knows how to listen.*

"Are these the major issues that you think you want to focus on or are there others we should consider?"

John strokes his chin and thinks for a few minutes. "Actually, there are probably 20 or 30 items that we should also talk about, but for the time being, these are a good place to start."

"That's a good thing," Aaron says with a laugh. "If there's one thing I know for sure, when I try to solve more than two or three things at once, nothing gets done. And most of the time, I think two or three things are too much."

Just as Aaron is about to continue, in barges John's son, Adam. Adam starts talking to his father without even looking to see who else is in the office.

Typical, John thinks, fuming. John glares at Adam. "Don't you ever wait until I say 'come in' before barging in?" he says. "I have a guest here. Whatever is on your mind is just going to have to wait."

Adam acts like he hasn't heard a word his father said. "If I didn't barge in," he snaps, "you wouldn't know that we sort of fixed the problem we had yesterday by getting product to XY Medical Devices. Or don't you remember that was the only thing you cared about before you went running out the door to that stupid chamber event."

John thinks about his options. He doesn't want Aaron to think he's a total jerk, so instead of talking to his son like usual, he tries to remain calm. "I'm glad we got the product to XY. But I still think you need to learn some manners. I'll get with you later today to see what we can do about making sure we don't have late shipments to our best customer again." It takes everything in his power to keep his tone even.

How a 25-year-old could be so obnoxious, he can't fathom. He thinks to himself, if this was anyone besides his son he would have fired Adam a long time ago.

Adam shrugs and leaves the office, slamming the door behind him.

John looks at Aaron. "You see what I have to put up with?" he says. "That's my son, Adam, on his best behavior. Now, where were we?"

Aaron recognizes one challenge already. First things first, he'll get to that dynamic later. He takes a breath, reiterates the first part of the conversation, and continues. "Let's focus on where you'd like to be," he says. "We're going to take all the items we talked about and you're going to ask yourself this question, 'If we were to get together three years from now, what would be happening if my life was totally great and everything was working better than I could have ever hoped for?' I want to know what a perfect world would look like for you."

John takes a big breath. He's still annoyed with Adam. "If I had my wishes, my relationship with my son would work. You know, he's very talented. Yet he just doesn't seem to get the human communication thing." He could go on and on about his son, but he decides to move along. "I wouldn't be worried about losing our best customer. In fact, they would be adding to the business they do with us, a lot more. Come to think of it, I wouldn't be feeling tired all of the time and my relationship with my wife would be great." John waves an imaginary wand, a gesture indicative of magical thinking. He's a practical man, not a daydreamer.

Aaron pauses. He's used to a healthy dose of skepticism. "I guess that would be a good place to start. I don't want to overload you right away." He leans forward. "Okay, let's move on to step three," Aaron continues. "What's the value to you if you solve the two or three most important things bothering you today? How would your world change if we

were able to successfully solve those two or three things? And what would it be worth to you, both psychically and monetarily, if you could solve them?"

John blinks. Sure, he knows how much money each customer represents, the income they bring in, but he has yet to put a cost on his problems. He considers the question a bit longer, then shrugs.

"Some of the answers will be easy to figure out," Aaron continues. "For example, if we can help you fix the sales problem that you mentioned on the phone that could be worth several hundred thousand dollars to you, every single year. Others, we'll need to think about. Another thing that might get fixed, for example, is your inability to take a vacation. That's important because your wife seems to have lost trust that you'll ever take a vacation with her, and she's getting angrier and angrier with that. What do you think might be the value in fixing that? What dollar amount might we put on it?"

John scratches his head. "I don't know," he says. "Hard to put a dollar amount on that. But it'd certainly be nice not to feel like I'm running into a buzz saw every time I walk in the door to my house."

Aaron pulls his glasses down his nose and looks over them. "I think that probably has some value to you," he says.

John leans back in his chair, looks out the window and is silent for a moment. To John, this feels like an hour. To Aaron, such a pause is something that he expects. It often happens when he asks the first two questions in the Alignment Conversation.

In his head, John starts a conversation with himself. *If Anne and I could stop fighting, I would come to work thinking about what I need to do here and not what I need to do to placate her. It would be nice to come to face the workday without thinking about my problems at home. But will Aaron's way work?*

John brings his gaze back to Aaron and says, "I really don't understand how only fixing two or three things will help bring everything else that's wrong back under control. It just doesn't sound right to me."

Aaron has heard this before. "I could just ask you to trust me on this," he says, "but I won't. I've not done an awful lot to earn your trust. Let's just leave it at this: If you can solve those top three things with or without me, wouldn't it make your life better and leave you room to deal with some of the other things on your list?"

John considers this. *That's a pretty good answer. Aaron doesn't sound like the other consultants and advisors I've talked with. He seems to be a pretty straight shooter, and he isn't trying to impress me with how smart he is.*

Once John returns his gaze, Aaron continues. "Again, if we were able to solve these problems, what would be the value to you?"

"If I could have these things go away, I know one thing for sure. I would sleep better at night. I can't tell you how often I wake up more tired than when I went to bed. This morning was one of them. As to the monetary value, that's hard to say. Not losing XY and even getting more business from them would probably keep our company from going out of business. I'm not sure how to put a value on that, but I can say for certain it would be worth a lot to me to stop worrying."

Aaron thinks for a second. "Sounds like there's a lot of value to be captured here. Have you ever tried to solve these problems before?"

"Sure, and you can see that I've not been very successful at this."

"Why do you think that's true?"

"I'm not really sure. It seems that when I've tried before, all my old habits kept kicking in. I need to control what happens here, and I just get in my own way. All the stuff I try to change sort of peters out. A new crisis appears and then I

have to deal with that instead of just working on what I want to do."

Aaron nods. "Things always get in the way. That's part of life. That's business. One of the most valuable roles I play with people I work with is one of thinking partner. That's where we think about options and look at what might work under the present circumstances. I'm not going to solve your problems but I can help you think about options and see if what you're doing or about to do serves you. One of my jobs is to help you prioritize what you work on and to say no to those things that fall outside of that area. I also know that we're going to have to be flexible because, if there is one thing that's true in privately held businesses, it's that priorities change by their circumstances. We don't want to be running from one fire to another. We do want to have a process for evaluating whether we're doing things that have the highest value for the least amount of effort. Does that sound like something you'd like?"

John feels hopeful. He shifts back and forth in his seat. "It does."

The conversation continues, and after talking for a while, John comes up with a list of three things to accomplish:

1. Getting John's business and profits growing again.
2. Enabling John to get away occasionally for two-week vacations.
3. Deciding what John should do about his son, Adam.

CHAPTER 4: **VALUES MATTER**

Before John and Aaron meet again, they talk on the phone. Aaron has supplied John with a long list of things he could be paying attention to in his personal life and business. When Aaron sent John the list, he also included a few instructions:

This list is one that's too big for us to even consider. Just look at it and use it as a tool to help jog your memory for additional things you might want to work on. I've found that these are the most important items for people like you. Feel free to come up with other items that aren't on the list.

A few days after Aaron sent his list to John, they have a phone call.

"Which of these things should top the list?" Aaron asks. "We have to find out what issues have the biggest bang for the buck, so we can do what I call an Objective Review of your company."

John is a little confused, "What exactly are we trying to accomplish with the Objective Review? It seems that you're just on a fishing expedition. I thought we agreed that we needed to focus on three things— getting my profits growing, enabling me to take two weeks off now and again, and figuring out what to do with my son."

Sitting on his phone with his headset on, Aaron gazes out the window. "I can see how you might feel that way. When other people have seen this list they often feel overwhelmed. But I want you to work on what's important to you, not what I think is important for you. I find that when you take control of what you're working on, you'll be more engaged and probably get more value.

"Remember when we talked about you being the expert at what you want in your life? This is where you start showing that expertise.

"Before we even discuss this list, we're going to start by focusing on the values that are important to you, how your personal values integrate with company values, and how we take the issues that you're facing and put them in the context of having your values lead the solution for the issues that you face."

John, still confused, decides to go along. "Okay," he says, "I'll let you take the lead here, I'm not sure what you're trying to accomplish, but what you've talked about so far has made sense to me." John decides to see where this Objective Review process is going and keep his options open if he feels he needs to pull the plug.

The next week, Aaron arrives at John's office to begin their day together. The men greet each other and they spend a few minutes chatting before they get down to business. Once again they meet in John's office. The two take the seats they had the last time they got together. Aaron likes this. It helps provide some ritual from meeting to meeting.

Aaron starts, "John, the first thing we're going to focus on is your personal values. We're going to review the values instrument I asked you to do and choose five values that you hold dear. We're then going to see how we can integrate your personal values into your company values. And, yes, I realize that you probably haven't explicitly told anyone here what those values are. We'll get to that a little later, I promise."

John squirms in his chair. "Okay, let's get started. I do think this values stuff is a little soft for me to get my arms around." He thinks to himself that this better have some real value for his company or he'll end up bailing.

Aaron continues. "Not only do we need to know what your values are, but we also need to know how they fit together and why they're important. What they mean to you. What they mean to your company. What they mean to your family." He waits a moment for John to process these words, to move beyond the inclination to attack his three biggest problems without understanding their root causes. "See, private businesses

like yours are defined by the personality of the owner. It's up to you to make sure employees are supporting the values you believe are important. They must adopt your values. If they do, they stay and prosper. If they don't, they go."

With Aaron's guidance, John quickly settles on three values he believes are vitally important: personal responsibility, financial security, and innovation. Aaron explains that the three chosen values will be at the center of the mission statement they will develop. He also tells John that not only does he need to identify the values that are important, but he also has to put together a clarifying statement for what they mean.

John tilts his head to one side. "What do you mean by a clarifying statement?"

Aaron returns John's gaze. "A clarifying statement is what your employees and you are going to use to know what each of the values mean. For example, when you say personal responsibility, you might know what it means. I'm going to bet that if you ask the first ten people that walk by your door for their definition, you'll hear ten different things. The clarifying statement is what will help everyone get on the same page."

"Can you give me an example of what a clarifying statement might look like?" John says.

Aaron thinks for a second and decides to use one of his own, instead of John's. "One of my values is simplification. For me, that value has a clarifying statement that says, 'Simplification takes the complicated and reduces it to an easily understood concept that any fifth grader could grasp.'" He pauses, stretching his long legs before him. "You see, simplification is something I hold dear. Too often people use jargon without an explanation. Or, they take simple things and make them complicated. I actively fight against both when I work with others and in my own life. But, let's get back to your values and what's happening here at Aardvark."

John can't remember the last time anything was simple at Aardvark. He explained the lack of cohesion to Aaron on

that first day, the feeling that his job was little more than herding cats. He shoots Aaron a look of defeat.

"Right now, all your employees appear to be doing their own thing, making it up as they go," Aaron says. "When we start taking your values and implementing them in your company, what do you think will happen?"

John scratches his head, looks around. "This is weird. I don't know."

"Some people are going to leave your company. They might even be important people. Are you okay with that?"

John looks worried. "I don't know," he says. "Some people I can't afford to lose."

"Okay, let's think about this for a second. If these people left, what's the worst that could happen?"

"I don't know. I guess I could lose all my customers and go out of business."

Aaron raises his eyebrow. "You really believe that could happen?"

"Probably not. But it could."

"Do we want to work with probabilities, or do we want to work with coulds and mights? It's up to you."

John is silent for a moment. Then he says, "We probably should deal with reality. Though anybody could leave at any time, the fact is nobody's departure but my own would probably cripple the company."

"Precisely. Your business is you, John. It needs to represent your visions and values, not anybody else's. You've never really been very thoughtful about how you communicate your values throughout Aardvark. I know this sounds harsh, but I bet you would admit that it's true."

Aaron already knows that what keeps Aardvark from prospering is John. Now he needs to help John come to the same understanding. This is something that Aaron knows will take time and it's one of the hardest things he helps his owner clients understand.

John doesn't think he's the problem. *What's all this nonsense with values, with getting everybody on the same page, with spending precious time on clarifying then communicating them?* He knows something has gone off the tracks, though. That's why he's sitting here talking to Aaron. John goes quiet for a few minutes and thinks about what running a values-led company might mean. The notion suddenly feels freeing. John turns his attention back to Aaron. Maybe the guy is on to something.

"Let's take a look at your top values of personal responsibility, financial security, and innovation," Aaron says.

The office door swings open, banging against the wall. Adam marches in, seemingly oblivious to the drama of his entrance. "Dad, you won't believe what just happened." He stands before the two men, ignoring Aaron. "You know that new warehouse person we hired?" He doesn't wait for an answer. "He's the one that screwed up the shipment to XY, and that's why they're mad at us." He spreads his legs and puts his hands on his hips. "I think we should fire him. We can't have someone that stupid hanging around here."

John glares at his son. He has no interest in making a scene in front of Aaron, but he can't contain himself. "Adam, again you don't knock. And again, you have no idea what you're talking about. I checked on that shipment. The reason it was late wasn't because of our new warehouse guy, it was because our finishing machine was once again broken and no one could find you to fix it. Get out of my office, right this instant. Can't you see I'm busy?"

Sneering, Adam turns on his heels and leaves. John gets up to slam the door shut. He sits back in his chair and lets out an angry grunt.

Aaron sees the teaching moment at hand. "John, what just happened here?"

"My son, Adam, he's a jerk. He's rude, inconsiderate, and forever looking for a scapegoat. I have to figure out what to

do with him. Maybe we should talk about that instead of all of this value stuff."

"We'll definitely get around to helping you come up with some strategies for working with or even not working with your son. For the time being, however, I'm hoping we can get back to our values conversation and move forward with this. I think you're going to find there's a method to my madness."

John looks out the window and thinks for a few seconds, then turns his attention back to Aaron and says, "Okay."

"Let's talk about personal responsibility, one of your top values. Your biggest complaint when we talked before was that people don't pick up the ball like they should, that you always have to correct them and take over the things that get dropped. And one of the reasons for this is that you're not stressing the importance of personal responsibility. You're not telling them that justifying and blaming will not get them anywhere. Your son is a brilliant example of this. You're allowing blaming and justifying to continue. It's your job to make sure it stops. Until you call foul when blaming happens, you're never going to have a company where people act in a responsible manner. Including your son."

John isn't quite sure how to respond. On one hand, he wants to justify his anger for his ridiculous son. On the other, Aaron may have a point.

Aaron continues, "Was Adam showing personal responsibility with his part of the conversation?"

John looks out the window again. "Clearly not."

"What could you have done differently that might create a different outcome?"

John starts to see what Aaron is getting at. "I could have had a conversation with Adam about the way he blames others."

Aaron knows there is a big difference between understanding you should use values as teaching tools and actually doing it. He decides to focus on how to use values to move the company forward. He's going to have to help John un-

derstand that he's the one who leads the problem with blaming others when things go wrong. He understands how John thinks the buck stops with him and at the same time he has seen John blaming and justifying why things aren't working at Aardvark. He also knows that getting owners to take responsibility for what happens in their company is often hard. It's a land mine that he's not ready to approach just yet.

"You have to be aware that when you use a values conversation for the first time," Aaron says, "your son and other members of your staff will probably not understand what you're talking about. In fact, I'll bet, like your son, your employees really don't listen to what you say. What they do pay attention to is your actions. They speak for themselves. So you're going to need to learn a new skill: You're going to have to match your words with your actions. This is a lot harder than you might think. Some people like to refer to this type of behavior as walking your talk. I think it's a good metaphor."

The conversation has been focused on the value of personal responsibility. Aaron knows that he needs to work fast and come up with some more ideas. Over the next hour, he and John flesh out the five values that they would use to focus Aardvark's employees and, for that matter, John, when it comes to behavior.

Aaron suspects that the values they are starting out with, and are identifying at the moment, will not be the five values that he and John will implement in the company. Aaron also knows that they have to start somewhere.

"Okay then," Aaron says. "Let's recap what we have now for values we want to emphasize: personal responsibility, financial security, innovation, rights and respect, and organizational mission. Personal responsibility fits in closely with rights and respect, or at least it appears that way to me. What do you think? One of the sayings you'll hear me say a lot is simplify, simplify, simplify—or, as Gino Wickman, the author of *Traction*, one of my favorite books, says, 'Less is more.'"

"You know, as an Eagle Scout," John says, "I learned it's important to have a mission that's bigger than you, one that helps other people. I also learned it's really important to respect other people's rights, just as I would expect others to respect mine."

"John, those are two interesting thoughts. Do you really think people around here are going to buy these as being what you really believe? After all, it seems from our first phone calls there is a trust issue between you and the rest of your staff. Or, at least that's what I've heard."

Aaron has touched a nerve. John has heard this statement to mean that he's irresponsible. No one calls John Aardvark irresponsible, not on his watch anyway. "I've always been really personally responsible, especially in how I run this company. You can't own a company and go around blaming other people or justifying your mistakes. You don't learn anything that way." When he sees no reaction play across Aaron's face, no defensiveness, John looks at the concept from a different angle. "And yet I've accepted other people doing these things, accepted it in my employees, without even realizing or thinking much about it—until now."

"Being personally responsible is a hard thing for everyone at first. Once you start exhibiting it in a congruent manner, your employees will get that you're serious. Are you ready for the next step?"

John pauses and thinks. *I see how this values stuff might be used in our company. I never thought about it before, but it might even make my life a little easier if I do this on a consistent basis.* He turns his attention back to Aaron.

This time John doesn't scratch his head; he nods vigorously. "Let's keep going," he says.

CHAPTER 5: **WALKING THE TRUTH**

After lunch, the two men return to John's office to continue their work.

"Okay," Aaron says when they are properly situated. "We're going to take your five values now and put them into context. We've got personal responsibility, financial security, innovation, rights and respect, and organizational mission."

"Context," John says, "What do you mean by context, exactly?"

Aaron smiles. John hadn't caught the word before in their previous conversation. Doing so now means he's starting to appreciate the nuances. "Values are tricky things. Too often we start talking about values, how people in the company will either believe you or not. For example, when you say financial security is a core value and you do it in context, will people believe you operate with that value in mind now?"

John glumly looks at his shoes. "We certainly aren't financially stable in the way I want now."

"Correct. So if you were to go out and start telling your staff that a core value you hold is financial security, they likely would not think you're telling the truth."

John digests this. "What should I be doing instead?"

Aaron spends a few seconds gathering his thoughts. He decides this is a good time to talk about the types of values that can exist in a company.

"John, one of my favorite authors is Patrick Lencioni. He's got a really good way of labeling the types of values that exist in companies. These values include:

Core Values—Values that exist in a company all of the time.

Aspirational Values—Values the company wants to have but don't exist yet.

Accidental Values—Values that you may not want to have but show up in a company.

Permission-to-Play Values—Values that exist most of the time but sometimes are not followed.

"I find that labeling these types of values helps you know what sort of work, if any, you need to do to make the values you identified core values. And to determine if you accurately label them. If you label them correctly and are honest about what types of values these are, your employees will believe what you have to say.

"Why don't we spend a few minutes and label each of the values we've been talking about? Based on the definitions I just gave you, are any of our five values core values?"

"Personal responsibility is."

"Really? That's a core value? Seems to me you have lots of people around here blaming and justifying and finding excuses for why things aren't being done or are being done wrong. Is that a core value of your business, or is it what we call an aspirational value?"

John looks at the ground again. This process is just as disquieting as he feared. "You know," he says, "I'm really disappointed in myself. I should realize that although personal responsibility for me is important, I've not required it of others in the company. I need to do that."

"Now, how about financial security? Is that a core value?"

"Probably that one's aspirational, too. We're not very successful at following it right now."

"Okay, how about innovation?"

"Ah," John says, brightening. "That's a core value. We do innovation really well."

"Great, but have you systematized it? Would your engineers be able to explain the steps that they take to create and innovate a process?"

"No. But what's that got to do with being a core value or not?"

"Labeling something a core value is a place to start. But without a system to ensure that it will endure, a value isn't much more than an idea. Soon you're going to get together with your head of engineering and make it a core value. Or, better yet, you're going to assign someone else to get together with the head of engineering. But, we're getting ahead of ourselves. We won't talk about systems just yet."

Both men fall silent for several moments.

"You mean I really have to let someone else do this?" John finally says. "As the owner, valuing personal responsibility, valuing innovation, shouldn't I be the one to drive these changes?"

"What do you think?"

"I guess I'll have to delegate some of this stuff out. But here's my question. If I'm not at the helm, if I'm not getting everybody on board with the changes we're proposing, what am I going to be doing? How am I going to spend my day? I mean, I'm really good at this innovation stuff, I really like doing it."

Aaron leans forward and adjusts his glasses. "Answer this," he says. "Do you want to have a sustainable company that's going to be around for another generation after you leave?"

"Of course. That's why you're here."

"Then doesn't your innovation process have to be successful when you're not here?"

John has never considered this notion before. He sits up in his chair. "You know, I guess you're right."

"Your job is to help make your company strategically excellent. My job is to help you think through this process."

"Okay, that's kind of a cool thing," John says. "I think I can deal with that. But I'm going to miss doing innovation. It's a core competency for me. It's my thing."

"If it's your thing, maybe we can find a way to make you part of the team, without the need for others to be dependent on you. And we have to make sure it's systemized; otherwise your business probably won't exist when you've moved on to what's next in your life."

John likes the sound of this.

Changing the subject slightly, Aaron asks, "Why do your customers do business with you?"

John has to think about this for a minute. He's never even thought about why people do business with his company. He turns back to Aaron, "It's because of our innovative processes for helping them solve their problems and for getting very complicated casting done that fits their products."

"You don't absolutely have to stop paying attention or even participating in this process. The truth is you won't for a while anyway. What you will need to move toward is having other people take the lead. This is a really difficult thing for founders to do. But, I'm not telling you anything you don't already know."

John feels light, as though a heavy weight has suddenly been lifted from his shoulders.

Time is getting short. Wanting to complete the core values conversation so they can implement, Aaron pushes on. "Now, how about rights and respect? Is that a core value?"

"Not really. Because it sort of fits in with personal responsibility, which isn't being done around here. I mean, I respect people around here, I think."

Aaron arches his eyebrow and looks at John. "Really? Do you always respect people?"

"Maybe not so much."

"And when you're not respecting the rights of others, how do you behave?"

"I kind of demean them. I call them idiots. I say they're not very smart. Then I take over their jobs." John feels embarrassed just by saying this out loud. He clears his throat.

"Which of those responses is most damaging?"

"Calling them idiots, probably." John frowns. "That has to be the most damaging."

"Really?"

"It's not? What is, then?"

Aaron studies John. "Think about it. How else do you disempower them?" He tilts his head to one side. He doesn't want to give too many hints, but he does want John to see the deeper implications.

"Would it be that I'm taking over their jobs?" John says.

"What do you think?"

"That probably sounds about right to me."

"Yeah, that sounds about right to me, too. So we have to classify that as a permission-to-play value. If you want to make it a core value, you'll have to put together some strategies for helping you and those around you change how you deal with showing respect to each other. You might even want to start with your son."

John feels bad. Yes, Adam is immature, inconsiderate, and undependable, but he's beginning to sense his role in it all. Saying he wants Adam to run with the ball, then taking it away from him, berating him the moment the play runs afoul. Sometimes ignoring a problem, sometimes making a big stink about it. *Permission to play, for sure.*

"Let's move to your last value, organizational mission. Doing big things that benefit the community, isn't that what you said it means to you?" Aaron is sure that part of John's definition came up in a previous conversation.

"That's absolutely an aspirational value," John says, "something I've always wanted do, but never have had enough money to do."

"That kind of fits in with financial security, doesn't it?"

"Sure does." The pieces are all beginning to click into place for John.

"Do you see that your top values are all linked together?"

"Yeah," John says, "Four out of the five, at least. Personal responsibility, financial security, rights and respect, and organizational mission fit together."

"That's a really good observation." Aaron leans back in his chair and rests the back of his head in his palms.

"How's that? You haven't said anything good yet today, so why're you starting now?" John doesn't know if he should laugh or be mad. He has never been good at being called out on the rug, yet he sees how understanding himself, what truly motivates him, may do some good.

Aaron senses that it's time to change gears, maybe wrap it up for the day.

"John, are you aware of all the work we just accomplished? And are you aware of how much mental energy you just used?"

CHAPTER 6: THE OBJECTIVE REVIEW CONTINUES

What would happen if we use values as a tool? *What would happen, what would happen, what would happen?* John mulls over Aaron's question. They've been at it for over an hour, having picked their conversation up from where they left off the week before.

Aaron sits patiently the entire time, not wanting to interrupt the valuable thought process.

"I'm going to have a great company that's going to become sustainable," John finally says. "My kids will be able to take it over. At least my daughter will. It remains to be seen what's going to happen with my son. Which really worries me a lot, by the way. But we'll get to that. I'm not sure we need to fire him. We can maybe just demote him."

"We're not there yet," Aaron says, "Let's talk about your son some other time. For now, let's get back to you. You have a core value in innovation. And in personal responsibility, financial security, rights and respect, and organizational mission, you have aspirational values and permission-to-play values that I believe can be turned into core values in less than six months, if you stay focused."

"How can I possibly do this in six months?" John asks. He's bought into the necessity of identifying his values, to walk his talk so others will do the same, thereby transforming them into core values. He also understands that he will not be able to solve his three biggest problems—getting his profits growing again, escaping for an occasional vacation with Anne, and deciding what to do about Adam—until he does just this. He knows old habits die hard and that it takes effort to turn the ship around. How much effort, he isn't sure.

Aaron spots the concerned look playing across John's face. "Why don't we take a little break and you can show me around this place," he says.

John perks up. He always seems to think more clearly when he's walking around. All of this sitting and talking is starting to make him antsy.

When they exit the office, they run into Janice, the operations manager, a tall woman in her mid-40s. She looks distressed. "John," she says, "we have a big problem. Our finishing machine is down again, and Adam is nowhere to be found."

John's face turns red. He almost blows up but, thinking better of it in Aaron's presence, he manages to retain his cool. "Janice," he says through gritted teeth, "I just don't have time to deal with that now. You need to find him, and you need to get him to fix that thing once and for all. I'm getting really tired of hearing about the same problem every day. And this is the third time today that thing's gone down, and it's not even noon."

Janice looks flustered. She glances at Aaron, clearly wondering who he is. Noticing Janice's confusion, John introduces Janice to Aaron. "We'll all be meeting with Aaron later in the day," John says, his tone betraying his annoyance. "I'm hoping that he can help us find some answers. I just can't keep dealing with these issues if we're ever going to make progress here."

"You see what I have to put up with," John says to Aaron once Janice retreats into the coffee room. "This happens every time I leave my office. Some disaster seems to be waiting for me all of the time." He isn't sure he has the heart to carry on with their tour of the plant.

"Why do you think this happens, John?" Aaron says.

Great. More questions. "Well," he says, "it's probably because everything here seems to run through me. Because of our conversation this morning, I'm starting to see this as a problem I need to fix."

The two abandon their tour at John's suggestion and return to his office. After his outburst at Janice, John thinks it might be a good idea for him to focus, to see what else Aaron needs to talk about.

By now, John and Aaron have claimed their own comfortable spots in the office. John collapses into his big, leather chair, where he can look at the window. Aaron flops down on the sofa so he can sprawl, as is his habit. John lets off a sigh.

"Remember we were talking about aspirational values becoming core values?" Aaron says. "In order for those values to move from the aspirational variety to the core, what would you have to be doing differently?"

"I'd channel you," John says with a snort.

Aaron laughs. "Yeah, that helps. Go ahead and channel me. What does that mean in the real world?"

"Maybe I'm going to learn to ask questions instead of telling people what to do."

"Have you ever asked questions of your employees?"

"Of course, I ask questions." Even to his own ears he sounds offended.

"What types of questions?"

John scratches his head. "Basically yes-or-no questions, I guess. I say, 'Will you do this?' And if the answer is no, I say, 'Why are you such an idiot?'"

"What do you think that does to the conversation?" Perfectly comfortable, Aaron stretches out his long legs on the couch.

John stares out the window and goes inside himself for a few minutes. He turns and looks at Aaron. "I guess it might be a show stopper, at least it would be for me. I know I hate being told what to do, having no choice in the matter, being insulted. Now that you've asked me this question, it seems obvious."

"You need to learn to ask open-ended questions. As you ask open-ended questions, you'll find that the people working with you will start reacting the same way you are with me. Does that make any sense?"

"Yes."

"What did I just do now, John?"

"You asked a yes-or-no question."

"Did that help you learn or accept?"

"No."

"But if I were to say, 'How is this going to impact what you're doing? How is this going to change what you're doing? How will this make your life different? How will this make your life better?' What kind of answer am I going to get?"

"I'd have to think a little more, and my response would be more interesting."

"When people who report to you make a mistake, what are you going do?"

"What do you mean?"

"Let's say you have a late shipment. What's the question you're going to ask?"

"I'm going to ask why we have a late shipment."

"What kind of response is that going to get you?"

"You know," John says, thoughtfully, "it's probably not going to get me the response I want. They'll probably get really defensive. They'll probably say, 'I don't know.'"

"Instead, if you were to ask a question that supported your values, what would that sound like?"

John scratches his head. "What prevented us from getting this shipment out on time?"

Aaron smiles. "And what value does that support?"

"It shows respect. And it kind of requires personal responsibility."

Aaron thinks maybe fixing Aardvark isn't a lost cause. "Yeah. If everybody did that in your company, how would the company look? Would it be a different company?"

"Oh, yeah. It would be a really different company."

John allows himself the slightest glimmer of hope that things could be different around his company. He sees that there might be a way to reach his major goals. *Identify core values, walk the talk, teach others to do the same.* He also knows that he's going to have to ask others for help, something he has rarely done. The idea of it alone makes him nervous. What if his employees fail him? What if they don't respond? What then?

He swings his attention back to Aaron, anxious to dive back in. "What's next on our agenda? We've dealt with core values and we've started to talk about aspirational values. How do we move aspirational values into the core value column?"

"It really comes down to being consistent in how you work with your people. You need to walk your talk and you need to ask open-ended questions that allow those you're working with to discover what they're doing wrong—or, for that matter, what they're doing right. You also need to admit that aspirational values are just that, aspirational. When you do this, you'll gain credibility with your people that you might not have had before. And, it's only because you're telling the truth."

"Got it. At least, the concept."

"Let's move on to two other types of values. Both are the sorts of values I don't like, but, boy, do they often exist. One is an accidental value."

John narrows his eyes. "Accidental value? I know you defined it before, but remind me."

"An accidental value is a value you really don't want to have, but somehow do. For example, you now have in place at the company the value of blaming others when something

goes wrong. You almost always blame somebody else. That's not a good value; it's an accidental value. Values like that, negative values, you need to kill. And killing a negative value would accomplish what?"

"That's an open ended-question," John says with a chuckle. "Very good."

"Okay, if you get rid of a negative accidental value, what's going to be different?"

"First, I have to identify the accidental values in our company."

"Yes, okay. What then?"

"Then I need to have a conversation with my management team and talk about values—core values and aspirational values and accidental values. And I need to get their ideas on how we can eliminate accidental values. I also need to start being the example." For the first time in a very long time, John feels the thrill that accompanies innovation, making things better, more efficient.

"Being the example, what does that mean?"

John thinks for a few seconds, "It means that the only way we're going to see different values exhibited and used is if I set the example. If I'm being really honest, it's something I've not always done properly."

"I'm impressed," Aaron says. "I like that. I think it will probably work. So that's a good step to take. It might even start to give your team an opening to see you in a different light."

John considers this idea. He tries to imagine Janice relaxed around him, and Adam being respectful. He's never needed to be pals with his employees, but it would be nice if they didn't cringe whenever he entered a room.

"Okay," Aaron says. "Let's talk about our last kind of value, the permission-to-play value. One of your five top values could be considered a permission-to-play value. A permission-to-play value is something that is often a uni-

versal value, one that get's ignored or fudged sometimes for the sake of convenience. In your case, it would be rights and respect. This is something we're going to need to pay attention to sooner, rather than later."

"Right." It's the end of the day. John is more than willing to move on.

"What do you think the problem is with a permission-to-play value like rights and respect, John?"

"No idea."

Aaron gives John an exasperated look. "Really? If you had to guess, what would you say?"

"Hmmm. I can tell you this. When I allow any form of disrespect to exist, we always seem to get caught. And it puts us in a really bad light with our customers."

"Right. Permission-to-play values also need to disappear. And what word do you need to learn, John, if you're going to get rid of accidental values and permission-to-play values?"

"A word? What about an action?"

"Actions come with it but there's a word you need to learn. That word is *no*. If you don't learn to say no, you're going to always have accidental values and permission-to-play values in your company. If you don't learn to say no, you'll always have the wrong customers in the company. If you don't learn to say no, you'll lose a lot of time doing the wrong things. If you don't learn to say no, all the stuff that we want you to delegate will to get dumped right back in your lap. And if you don't learn to say no, you'll remain stuck where you are right now. In my experience, almost every time a business gets stuck—and your business, John, is stuck—it's because the word *no* isn't being used enough."

CHAPTER 7: **THE VENERABLE MISSION STATEMENT**

"We have one more thing to do today and two more things we're going to talk about. The one thing we're going to do is develop a mission statement," Aaron says, hoping to keep John focused for another hour. He recognizes the look of someone who has had enough: head rubbing, foot tapping, and a fixation with items on one's desk. John is displaying all of these signs. "What is it that you do for your customers that's really valuable?"

"We create innovative processes," John says from behind his desk. He's moved there just to mix things up, to play with some of the toys he has on his desk.

"Yes. But doesn't that sound like something everybody in the world does?"

"It does."

"So, is that a reason for someone to do business with you?"

"Well, I..." John squeezes the bridge of his nose.

"Is that something your production people can grab hold of and say, 'This is something I'm willing to get behind?'"

"I guess we need innovation out there, don't we?"

"Yes, we do. And what else?"

He spots a customer appreciation plaque hanging by the door, which inspires an idea. "How about, 'We make our customers' lives easier'?"

Aaron says, "Let's see, that's one, two, three, four, five, six words. That's certainly less than the 10 you need for an effective mission statement. Anything longer that and no one

remembers it. Okay. Is making your customers' lives easier something that's important to you?"

"Yes. Of course."

"Does it open up a range of things you can do for your customers that you might not be doing right now?"

"You know something? It does." A few possibilities cross John's mind. *Make a customer's life easier, and they'll keep coming back time and time again.*

"Is it something that can be answered with a yes or a no, meaning you are doing it or not doing it?"

"Definitely. We're either making our customers' lives easier or we're making them harder, there's not anything in between."

"That could be something we might start using as a mission statement. And to let you know, the first crack we take at a mission statement isn't always the last. You don't have to be stuck with what you choose first. At the same time, I do think this is a really good start."

"The mission statement we have right now is two pages long, and, frankly, I can't remember what's in it," John says. "You read it. Do you remember what's in it?"

"I stopped reading after the first paragraph," Aaron says. "It was just gobbledygook to me. And I knew where we were going to go with this process, so I said to myself, 'Why bother?'"

"Here's the deal with your mission statement. When you start to use it with your people, you're going to feel awkward. You're also likely to get pushback because it's too generic. Just remember that less is more and simple usually is more effective than complicated.

"One of my favorite quotes is from Peter Drucker. He says, 'The purpose of a business is to create a customer.' I wouldn't say that's very complicated, but it is complete and does explain what a business needs to do. I would put your

new mission statement into the Drucker column in that it's easy to understand and simple."

The end of the first day looms. Aaron knows he needs to tie up the day and give John some homework. "Okay, John," he says, "next time we get together, I want you to have supporting statements for your mission statement—the one that says, 'We make our customers' lives easier.'

"I'll also need to have you use your mission statement at least five times a day in various contexts and let the people you're talking with know how the conversation you're having with them integrates with that mission. And ask, 'Are we doing it, or are we not doing it?' Because sometimes we make our customers' lives easier, but most of the time we don't. And the reason for this is that we think it's easier to do a short-term fix instead of the right thing. That might be true in the short run but in the long run, it's never true. Does that make sense?"

"Oh, I get it," John says. "Life gets easier for our customers, which makes them happier with us, and we actually have something to talk about with prospective customers, something that could be incredibly valuable to them."

"You're starting to get it," Aaron says. "And there's something else that's really important. I want you to talk about the 'how' in your mission statement. In other words, when you're saying 'Our purpose is to make our customers lives easier,' you have to have specifics on how you are or aren't doing it."

John imagines having this conversation with Stan, Adam, Janice, and the rest of his staff. He has a hard enough time being understood without bringing mission statement language into the mix. "How, ultimately, will I hold everyone to the mission? I don't want to look like a dork."

Aaron replies, "My first mentor taught me a couple of things when I was first in business and too young to know anything. He taught me the term 'operationally doable.'

This just means that for something to be done, it has to be simple."

John sighs. To his way of thinking, very few tasks at Aardvark Manufacturing resemble rocket surgery. But maybe he has been making things more difficult than they need to be.

Aaron gets that John is done for the day. He wants to get one more quick point in before they quit. "John, there's one more short thing I want to talk with you about before we stop. Do you remember the conversation you had with Janice this morning?"

"Yes," John says, glancing at his watch.

"You told her what to do, right? What could you have done differently?"

"Maybe I could have asked her a question?" John says.

"And what would that question have been?"

"Janice, have we had this problem before?"

"And Janice would have likely just said 'yes.' What would have been your follow-up question?"

"What can we do differently so this doesn't happen again?"

Aaron once again smiles. "What do you think her answer would have been this time?" he says.

"She might have said, 'We need to have a better system in place to make sure these machines work and aren't dependent on one person being around to fix the problem,'" John says.

Aaron allows himself a sense of victory. "John, what did you just do?"

"I used a question that was open-ended that allowed her to be responsible and that gave me something I could follow up on. Actually, we do need a system around here to follow through when Adam starts one of his disappearing acts."

"John, it looks like Janice made a mistake and you made sure she paid for it."

John furrows his brow and looks uncomfortable. "I hate mistakes," he says. "Mistakes stink. Nobody should make a mistake."

Aaron looks at John and says, "John, tell me something. Did you ever learn anything when you did it right the first time?"

John laughs. "No. It always took me a couple of times to get it right."

"Okay, so if you did stuff wrong, you would call that what?"

"A mistake," John says sheepishly.

"Okay, when you made a mistake what happened next?"

"I guess I learned something."

"Okay. Are you unique? Or is that how everybody learns?"

"Hmm," John says. "That might be one of my problems. I've always thought I was different than the rest of my people. That's not right."

"John you're making some progress," Aaron says. "Running up against your own management mistakes can be pretty uncomfortable. But I've got to tell you, at the outset of my business career, I was the world's worst manager. All the things you're doing wrong, I once did to a factor of 100. I screamed at employees who made mistakes. I called them every name in the book, using very colorful language in the process. I thought they were trying to screw with me. I thought they were trying to take advantage of me. And, like you, I believed the problem was them; that I had no part in what was going wrong.

"My problem was a control issue. During my fourth year in business, I opened a second branch operation. Going from one branch operation to two made me feel as though I wasn't able to manage every little thing. But if you want to grow a business, you can't micromanage it. You have to learn

to allow mistakes to happen. I know I did. My big mistake was that I never tolerated mistakes in others because I didn't know how to trust them. I didn't know how to allow my employees to make mistakes and learn from them. And we'll get to that whole trust thing soon enough."

John sits back. He appreciates the insight into Aaron's past. It makes him feel less the fool.

"It's getting dark outside. It's time to end for the day."

Aaron looks at John. "What do you think about our session today?"

"It was great. I do have to tell you though—I think I hated almost every minute of it."

CHAPTER 8: **THE CORE VALUE ANALYSIS**

At 8 o'clock the next morning, Aaron arrives at Aardvark. The receptionist escorts him to John's office. Aaron knows today is going to be stressful. He's going to help John and his team do an analysis of strategic areas in the business. Half of these will be internal activities and half will be externally focused areas.

Aaron has 30 minutes before the management team is scheduled to meet, just enough time to complete the tour of the plant he started the day before. He walks into John's office and asks to do so.

John is distracted. Once again, he's had words with Anne over their son, Adam. He's tense. He glances up from his desk, pushes his chair back and grunts. "Okay, let's go."

John and Aaron head down the hall to the manufacturing floor. "Why don't you tell me a little about each of the people we'll have at the meeting?" Aaron says.

John stops at the entry to the factory floor and gives Aaron safety glasses and earplugs.

"Let's start with Stan," John says once they're past the factory door. "You met him yesterday. He's been with me for years and does an okay job as long as I point him in the right direction. I have to follow up more than I want to and make sure things happen correctly."

"Janice, you met briefly yesterday. She's only been with us a few months. She was the production manager at one of our large competitors and wanted to get off the 80-hour-a-week treadmill she was on. So far, she's been a real find."

"Do you think Janice could take on more responsibility here?" Aaron says.

"Sure," John says. "In fact, I would love to see if we can integrate her into a more responsible position. Then there's my daughter, Alicia. She just finished her MBA last year and is going to be taking over our marketing department. And, finally, there's Fred, our controller. He's been with me almost since I started the company."

"What about your son, Adam?" Aaron says. "Isn't he an important part of the group?"

John begins slowly. "He is an important part of the company. But as I've told you, he's so disruptive I don't like to have him come to these types of meetings. If you want him there, I can ask him to attend." John still wants to solve the Adam problem. He doesn't want to get so waylaid by the process Aaron is taking him through to forget about that outcome.

Aaron thinks for a minute. Then he says: "Yes, I think he would be an important addition. I want to see how your entire team works with each other."

The two men enter the din. Dirt and dust fly everywhere. They stop at the smelter where a lineup of sand castings waits to be run through the pouring process. Aaron notices clutter around the smelter. In an offhand manner, he says, "John, what's the story with all of this clutter? It seems like your guys are walking over and around everything."

John looks at the clutter as if seeing it for the first time. "I've talked with them about this a bunch of times," he says. "It seems nothing ever gets better in this part of the plant."

Past the smelting room, they come to the finishing room, where Adam is bent over the buffing machine that was broken the day before.

John signals his son to come over. "Isn't that the same problem you had yesterday, Adam?" he says.

"Yeah," Adam says. "What's it to you?"

John glares at Adam. "You better lower your voice and change your tone," he says. "You might think this is okay to

do when you're at home, but it's not okay here. You need to get this fixed and then get your butt into our meeting. It starts in ten minutes."

Adam shrugs and goes back to working on the troublesome machine, muttering, "I'll get to your damn meeting when I can."

Aaron looks at his watch. "John," he says, "it's time for us to get to the meeting room. One of the things we need to establish is that meetings start and end on time. We can't set a bad example by being late. Remember, you set the tone of the company and it's by your example that everyone takes their cue for how to behave."

John and Aaron hurry out of the plant and into the main conference room. Aaron knows there is going to be some learning opportunities that happen. Some of them will be for the senior staff, but the really important ones will be for John.

Janice is already there. Aaron looks her way and says: "Hi, Janice. It's good to see you today. Hopefully today will be better than yesterday."

Janice smiles weakly. "I'm also hoping we have a better day."

Aaron looks around. He notices that there are really nice pictures on the wall of the plant looking pristine, along with a beautiful table and very comfortable seats. The conference room reminds him of one that you might find in a very nice law firm, not a blue-collar manufacturing plant. The conference room has a completely different feel than the rest of the plant. It's quiet and clean. Aaron thinks that bringing some of that cleanliness to the rest of the plant would be a really good idea.

In walks Stan. Aaron walks over and greets the salesman. "Hi, Stan," he says. "We never had a chance to be formally introduced. I'm looking forward to hearing your perspective

of how things work here and what we can do to improve our sales outlook."

Stan looks down and shrugs. "I sure would like to see us move forward," he says. "It feels like we've been stuck in the same place for a long time. I'm hoping you can help."

Alicia, John's daughter, and Fred, the controller, enter the room. John gathers everyone, introduces Aaron, then turns the meeting over to Aaron.

"The reason we're all here today is to review what I call value drivers in your business," Aaron says. "We're going to review nine internal value drivers and nine external drivers. Our purpose will be to find low-hanging fruit. In case you're interested, low-hanging fruit are things we can do that are relatively easy to accomplish and have a high payoff. Low-hanging fruit are those changes we can make within the company that will give us the biggest bang for the buck, for the least amount of effort.

"John is used to hearing me talking about values. But these are different. I'll tell you what I mean.

"Think of a value driver as something that drives the economic success of a business, a kind of system, something replicable. There's a difference between an internal value driver—things that happen inside the company—and an external driver—something that happens outside the company, for example, market share. Both are vital to the health of a company.

"First, we're going to spend a couple of hours going over the internal value drivers, take a break, and then dive into the external drivers. The outcome we're after today is to find two or three company-wide projects, which I call Big Rocks, that we'll commit to taking on. One of you will become the owner of each of these 'rocks,' and it won't be John.

"Let me give you a definition of a Big Rock. It's a project that's important and moves the company towards a particularly important goal. Too often Big Rock type projects are

lumped in with all the other things you have to do. Because you don't plan for Big Rocks first, they're often not completed. When we identify our Big Rocks today, I'm going to ask you to plan for moving them forward first, then plan for all of the other things you need to do after. If you do this, you'll find that you move towards completing Big Rock projects more quickly, which will help Aardvark move towards it's goals that much faster. If we do this, everyone should benefit."

Aaron eyes John, who is sitting back and watching. "Right, John?"

"Yup," John says. "That's right. I'm done doing work that you guys should be doing." He chuckles to himself and wonders whether he's going to be able to keep his hands off projects others take on. He knows he has a hard time trusting others to do their jobs. Aaron has certainly made that all the more evident.

All of the other people in the room look away once John tells his "joke." John thinks he's being funny, but as far as Aaron is concerned, this is one more example of his inability to appreciate other people's feelings. Aaron looks at John, scowls, and makes a mental note that before leaving today he must have a talk with John about his humor. Nobody appreciates snark.

Aaron hands out a worksheet with each of the nine drivers on them. The worksheet has a score box for how the company is doing, valued from 1 to 10; a section for general comments; and a place below for specific action steps. Aaron tells the group, "Not all nine drivers will have each area filled out—only those that Aardvark will take on as Big Rocks. Only those that Aardvark chooses to focus on." Each manager will take on one or two things in their area that will help improve Aardvark in a way that will have a strong positive effect on the company, its service offerings and, hopefully,

profits." Aaron then defines each of the internal value drivers and what they would look like if done properly:

Company: An outsider can easily get a holistic understanding of the company. This includes Aardvark's culture, practices, performance, disciplines and mission.

Financial: All of Aardvark's financial practices are in order, and the company follows best practices for putting together financial reports and controls.

Marketing: Aardvark has repeatable processes allowing potential customers to find the company easily and then figure out whether or not Aardvark can help them solve their need for high-end casting products.

Operations: Aardvark has the ability to deliver on sales promises made to the marketplace and do so in a systematic and process-driven manner.

Customer Satisfaction: Aardvark tracks and uses customer satisfaction metrics to meet customer expectations at all levels. They also have a working customer advisory board in place.

Management: Aardvark has a leadership team in place to realize the company's vision and mission while helping John achieve his objectives.

Human Resources: Aardvark has the ability to find, develop and retain quality people who enable success in all aspects of the business. This includes having a hiring system that provides regular success in hiring.

Legal: Aardvark has all of its legal affairs in order, including contracts and other agreements with outside organizations and employees. All are well-documented and kept up-to-date.

Innovation: Aardvark employees understand that innovation is invaluable to having a competitive advantage in the marketplace. Aardvark has a proven and systematic way to drive and capture new ideas and products, which encourages more innovation.

Aaron gives everyone ten minutes to review the definitions of the internal value drivers. Then he says, "Now, I would like all of you to rate Aardvark's performance in each of these areas on a scale of 1 to 10, with 1 being the lowest and 10 being the highest. I'm going to give you 15 minutes to go through and fill out your forms, and then we'll review the top three low-scorers on everyone's list; the areas Aardvark does exceptionally poorly in. I also want you to find the one thing on your list that Aardvark does at a high level. You might find we decide to focus on what we're doing well as the biggest opportunity, or you might want to focus on what we need to improve."

At the end of 15 minutes, Aaron looks at Alicia and asks her to list the three areas on the list that she thinks requires the most work. He then asks her to let the others know which area she thinks represents the best opportunity for company growth and improvement with the least amount of work.

"I think we need lots of work in marketing," Alicia says. "I gave that a 3. I also think it would be almost impossible for an outsider to understand what our company is about. I gave that a 2. I think management is a real problem here. All we do is fight with each other and my father. I gave that a 4. My highest rating was for innovation. I think we do a great job there and I gave us an 8."

John starts to talk, but Aaron gives him a stern look. "John, we're not discussing our ratings yet," he says. "I want everyone to have a chance to give us their opinion, and then we'll talk about our findings."

John is unhappy, but decides to keep quiet and see how this all plays out.

Aaron turns to Stan and says, "It's your turn now."

Stan nervously looks at his paper. "My worst on the list was company. When I talk to potential customers, I have a really hard time explaining who we are and what we do. I gave that a 2. My next worst was satisfaction. I get a lot of

calls from our customers complaining about late deliveries. I gave that a 4. And I gave innovation a 9. I think that's the best thing we do."

Stan sits back in his chair, glances at John out of the corner of his eye, and puts his head down. Aaron nods at Stan and says, "Thank you."

Aaron turns to Fred. "It's your turn now."

Fred clears his throat and glances at John. He's no doubt waiting for John to explode. He's been on the receiving end of more than one of John's outbursts, Aaron guesses. Everyone in the room seems to be on edge. John's outbursts about XY and the shipping problems the company has been having with the customer would be common knowledge. That's the way all of these companies work.

"I want to start with what I think we do best," Fred says. "Like Alicia and Stan, I also think it's innovation. I gave us a 9 there. My worst rating was company. I gave that a 2. Frankly, everyone around here seems to have their own agenda. We're never on the same page. It's almost as if everyone thinks they know what's best for the company and thinks everyone else is wrong. My next worst rating was for operations. We don't have very good systems, and as a result we spend a lot of time reinventing the wheel. I gave that a 4, and that might be too high."

Aaron thanks Fred and, holding his breath, turns his attention to Adam. "You're up now," he says.

The tension in the room suddenly becomes thick enough to cut with a knife. Clearly, everyone expects Adam to be nasty. He doesn't disappoint.

"I'm not even sure why we're doing this," he says. He looks at his father. "Dad, you've done lots of dumb things, but this might be the dumbest ever."

John's face reddens and he begins to yell. "Adam, get the hell out of here. And while you're at it, why don't you just

pack your bags and go home for the day. I'm really sick of your attitude."

Adam storms out of the room. The rest of the participants fall silent.

Aaron knows he better do something fast. He knows this show of dysfunction needs to be dealt with before continuing. "In the very near future," he says, "we're going to have a conversation about having the right people in the company doing the right things. John, it seems to me that you and Adam have some really hurtful conversations. Why don't we plan to spend some time on this before I leave today?"

John nods but is clearly seething. Inside, he's ready to disown his son, despite the trouble it would cause with Anne. He's ready to fire everyone in the room and move to Miami. And he doesn't even like Miami.

"John, do we need to take a short break?" Aaron says.

"No," John says. "We don't have a lot of time. We're going to have to keep going."

Aaron decides to override John and says, "John, you and I are going to the cafeteria for a cup of coffee. Everyone, let's be back here in 20 minutes. I'm sorry but we need to clear the air before we continue."

John and Aaron walk to the break room. There's no one there. Aaron looks at John, "What are you feeling now?" Aaron asks.

"I just want to kill my son. All he does is get under my skin. I would love to have him leave the company except he's the only one who can keep some of our machines running and Anne would have my scalp if I ever fired him."

Aaron thinks for a minute, takes a sip of coffee. "We don't have time to deal with this today, but I think we're going to have to handle this problem and handle it soon. I don't know if you notice how disruptive he is with all of the people in your organization. If you don't solve the Adam problem, I

can guarantee that Janice is going to leave your company, and right now she's way more valuable than Adam is."

John nods. He's intent on solving his three biggest problems—figuring out what to do about Adam, getting away on vacation with Anne, and having his business and profits growing. By now he knows the path to freedom will not be a straight line. "I'm going to let you talk with Anne about this. There should be some good fireworks. I'm ready to get back to the meeting if you are. I think I've calmed down enough to continue."

While they're walking back to the conference room, John finds himself deep in thought. He rarely, if ever, brings Anne into conversations about what's going on at the company. He realizes that he spends a lot of time complaining, but almost no time talking with her and asking her opinion. He decides that he needs to talk with Aaron about this before he leaves for the day. John wonders whether having a real conversation with Anne about Adam might help with this problem.

John and Aaron return to the room. All of the managers are seated. The bad air has seemingly dissipated. Aaron looks at the clock and notices 40 minutes have gone by. Before they continue the exercise, he decides a short conversation about Adam's outburst would be appropriate.

"We all just saw what happens when you allow somebody to try to bully a meeting," he says. "In my experience, outbursts like Adam's are as unproductive as anything you can have in a business. If anybody in any of your meetings acts the way that Adam did, I would encourage you to ask them to leave and then have a private one-on-one conversation after your meeting is done. We all know that Adam is a special case and will have to be dealt with. At the same time, if any of your people follow his lead, you're going to have to deal quickly with that type of issue.

"What you've seen here is what I call a Potential Wrong Person Conversation. It's this type of conversation that can

help you decide whether you have the right person in the company. I can assure you that John and I are having that conversation now about Adam."

John stares at Aaron the way he would a crazy man. He has no intention of letting him air his dirty laundry in front of his entire staff. Aaron takes note of John's horrified expression as he speaks. They'll have to address this issue. "For you folks at Aardvark to be successful," he continues, "you must be able to have open and honest communication. This includes communications that are uncomfortable or even embarrassing.

"John, I see that you're angry with me and, in a way, I don't blame you. The reason I brought this up is because we have an elephant in the room. Everyone here, including you, knows that your son is a problem. In some respects, he fits into the category of what I call the brilliant jerk."

John scowls. Yet, his curiosity outweighs his anger. "Brilliant jerk, what's that?"

"That's when you have someone in the company who is unbelievably talented and at the same time causes havoc. Everyone in the company spends most of their time trying to avoid him. In Adam's case, you've allowed him to behave like this. I know this is harsh, but it's true and everyone around this table knows it. They're just not willing to confront you about it. You and I will deal with this issue later, but it's important for your team to know that we know there's a problem that needs to be taken care of."

John is not used to being called out on his behavior, particularly in front of his staff. But he can feel all eyes on him. He knows that what Aaron is saying is true. He decides to sit with the comment, rather than protest, for the moment.

"Now let's get back to our analysis of the business." Aaron turns to Janice. "Are you ready to go?"

Janice nods, then goes through her internal driver ratings. John follows. For the most part, their answers jibe with

the rest of the management group. When they are through, Aaron defines the nine external value drivers in the form of questions:

Growth: Does Aardvark have a history of consistent growth greater than its competitors coupled with projected future revenue growth above the market rate?

Market Size: Does Aardvark's market support significant growth for the business?

Market Share: Does Aardvark own the highest percentage of the available market relative to its competitors?

Revenue: Can Aardvark rely on a portion of future revenue from contractually committed customers?

Barriers: Are there significant obstacles facing a new entrant into Aardvark's market?

Differentiation: Does Aardvark have a product or service with unique characteristics that provides a competitive advantage?

Brand: Does Aardvark have a recognizable brand that reinforces the business's presence in the marketplace and supports the company's objectives?

Margin: Does Aardvark enjoy gross and net margins greater than the industry norm?

Customers: Does Aardvark have a well-diversified customer base?

As with the internal value drivers, Aaron has the Aardvark leadership team rate each of the nine drivers on a scale 1 to 10 and then asks each of them to talk about his or her three lowest picks and the one strongest.

"Stan, why don't you start this time around?" Aaron says.

"I think our best area is market size," he says. "We can really grow this company if we learn to crack the code.

"Now, on to the three areas I think we need to improve on. I think our worst area is growth. We just haven't grown much over the last five years. I gave this a rating of 1. Then, it

seems to me that our gross margin has been steadily dropping, along with our sales stagnating. And, finally, John keeps telling me we need more customers because we have a few customers that do too much business with us. He also keeps telling me that this customer concentration issue could kill the company."

Aaron thanks Stan and turns to Fred, the controller. "Your turn now," he says.

"I'm not sure that I'm qualified to have an opinion on this," Fred says. "I really don't deal with any of these outside things on the list."

Aaron scratches his head. "You know, Fred, you see what goes on around here and I'm sure you have opinions, and that's all I'm asking for now."

"Okay," Fred says. "I guess the best thing we do on this list are the barriers to get into this business. I gave that a 6.

"As to the thing we can improve, I think the biggest problem we have is our customer concentration issue. If we lose one of these big customers, I wonder whether we'll be able to stay in business. I gave that a 1."

Aaron thanks Fred, then moves on. "Janice, what do you think?"

"I think the best news for us is that we have a really big market that we're not taking advantage of. If we even get one percent of this market, we're going to have a huge business. I give this opportunity a 10.

"As to the things we need to work on, they all have a 2 in my mind—and here they are: customer concentration, margin and brand, which also includes differentiation. I think we need to work on a strategy to improve our margin, because the work we do is really customized, and we get terribly underpaid for it."

Aaron thanks Janice. "Alicia," he says, "it's your turn now."

Alicia decides to skip the good things and go straight to the bad. "I think we really need to focus on our improvement areas," she explains. "For me, the areas we need to improve on are brand, differentiation, and margin. I don't know why everybody here is concerned about customer concentration. After all, haven't these customers been with us for years and years? I give brand a 1, differentiation a 3 and margin a 4."

Aaron scratches his chin and thinks, *Alicia really needs to learn about threats that could damage the company.* Although Alicia has an MBA, Aaron knows that in a small company new MBAs often provide more of a threat than a contribution. He has seen MBAs take simple ideas and make them too complicated to be used in the company. In this case, not seeing the threat from customer concentration is something he believes she should have learned. He decides to chalk up that comment to her youth and not her education.

Aaron knows that he'll have to work on Alicia's world view about customer concentration, but not right now because there are too many big things to work on at the moment. It appears there's a terrible lack of focus at Aardvark. They need to be focused on a workable group of projects that can actually get done.

"Alicia, it's really important that you choose something from this list that we do well," he says.

"If I have to choose something," she says, "I would agree with Janice and say that market size is our biggest advantage We don't have a large share of the market, which means it's a great opportunity that I would love to see us take advantage of."

"I guess it's my turn now," John says, calmer now. "Like Alicia and Janice, I think market size is our biggest opportunity; I gave that a 10.

"As to the things I worry about, number one on my list is customer concentration. Stan and I have been arguing about this for years. If we lose one of our big customers like XY,

we could be in big trouble. In fact, if we did, I'm not sure we could survive it. I gave this issue a 1. I also think this is the real thing we need to focus on and fast. It's what keeps me up at night.

"I then look at our revenue and the way it has stagnated over the past several years. This is part of our customer concentration issue. If we had more revenue, it would have to come from new customers—and without new customers we're stuck with this customer concentration issue. I also gave this a 1.

"And then there's differentiation. This is a really frustrating thing for me. I've just not been able to figure out what we can do to have potential customers see us as something different from the rest of the industry. I gave this a 2."

Aaron thanks everybody. "This has been a really hard three-and-a-half hours," he says. "We have 30 minutes left. Let's see if we can put a list together of the things that we need to work on."

While everyone goes through their lists, Aaron writes the earlier comments on a whiteboard.

"The biggest things I heard during the discussion on internal issues were company and operations," he says. "The biggest problems that came up for the external drivers were customer concentration and margin."

Aaron also notes that the two biggest things Aardvark does well are innovation as an internal driver, and the potential a huge market provides as the external driver. He knows that he will have to focus Aardvark on both the good things that they can take advantage of, and the bad things which need to be fixed. Such a one-two punch will greatly improve business, and allow John to become operationally irrelevant. Finally, John will be able to step away from the day to day operations of the company.

He turns from the whiteboard and addresses the team. "We've worked really hard today on all of these problems

and opportunities. I want to make sure that we don't just focus on things that need to be fixed. Often, focusing on opportunities has a much stronger result for a company than working on weaknesses.

"The next time we get together, we'll decide how many of these projects we have the capacity and time to deal with. We also want to figure out what the low-hanging fruit is—those changes we can make that will give us the biggest result for the least amount of effort."

The meeting adjourns and John walks Aaron out to his car.

"You know, you really embarrassed me in there," John says.

"I know," Aaron says. "I did it on purpose. Your staff seems to be terrified to take you on. And I see there's a good reason for that. If you react to negative news with your employees the same way you reacted to negative news with me, I can see why nobody wants to tell you the truth.

"You think that the solution to your problem is to have your hands in everything, to micromanage, to play gruff leader, someone who can't be questioned. But that's actually your problem. If you ever want to have a sustainable business, to be able get away for a couple of weeks, you've got to change your ways.

"If you decide that I'm not the guy for you, I'll understand. At the same time, I would like you to consider the possibility that this is something that's keeping your people from telling you the truth. And if they don't tell you the truth, there's no way you can build a great company. The choice is yours."

John is tempted to fire Aaron on the spot. But there's a little voice in his head telling him Aaron has a really good point. He decides he really needs to continue because of the problems he's facing.

After a long pause, John turns to Aaron, looks him in the eye and says, "No, I'm not going to fire you. As much as I hate what you did in there, it probably will be good in the long term. For way too long, people around here have been scared of me. You obviously aren't, and that might give some of the other people here the courage to speak up.

"Janice is new here, and, frankly, if I use my old behavior when I work with her, she's going to quit. And I just can't afford to have that happen."

Aaron opens his car door and gets in. Before he turns on the ignition, he looks at John and says, "John, this is really hard stuff you're going through. I know you don't believe this, but I was at the same place myself about 30 years ago. If I didn't change my behavior, my business would have gone bankrupt. I appreciate the dilemma you have. I'm also very thankful that you're showing me enough trust to continue down this path together. I think at the end of the process, you're going to be really happy with the result."

With that, Aaron drives away, wondering where all of this is heading.

CHAPTER 9: BIG ROCKS AND THE $5,000 PER HOUR JOB

Aaron stands up and leans against John's desk, looks at him for a few seconds and says, "John, let's talk about the Big Rocks we identified in yesterday's meeting. While each of your management team has committed to a special project, I need to remind you that everybody will need to depend on everybody else, not just you. Everybody has to get up in the morning and make it to work to do their job for the day to flow smoothly. Now, we know that employees have a hard enough time doing their regular job, without adding projects. Your employees are going to have, at the very most, 5 to 10% of their time available to work on these strategic projects. That's why we only assign one Big Rock at a time for them to work on, to avoid overwhelm.

"All these Big Rocks we've identified must be rolled into place before we can do anything else. And we need to have some sort of a reporting system whereby you, John, are going to know things are moving along on all these strategic fronts. You must supervise and inspect the work of every employee who reports directly to you. Not manage the projects, but inspect what's been done to make sure it's on track. And, if it's not on track, you can't fix it. You must, and I mean you *must*, have your managers solve their problems. It's the only way you're going to become operationally irrelevant.

"Regular and ongoing strategizing is required to take a successful business and make it sustainable. For you to move to operational irrelevance, you need to increase that 5% of strategic time to at least 50%. It's fine for your employees to devote this incremental amount of time to Big Rock tasks, but you'll need to devote half your day. This means you're going to have to choose the right things to work on and

delegate properly. Are you seeing how this all starts to fit together?"

The thought of anything taking up 50% of his day makes John cringe. He isn't sure how he's going to do that. Suddenly, the idea of Big Rock projects seems far less appealing. Even Aaron admits he'll have to oversee them. He says nothing, though, knowing that Aaron will explain.

Aaron continues. "What I want to see you do now is start a list of the day-to-day things you're going to give up. That way we can talk about the Holy Grail, operational irrelevance, which is what we're going to make you. If you want to be able to take an occasional vacation with your wife, this will be what allows you to do that.

"John, operational irrelevance is where you are completely out of the day-to-day operations of your business. This is where you focus on strategic activities and let Janice focus on the tactical stuff that needs to be done. It's what allows you to work less, enjoy what you do more and spend time the way you want to spend time, not on what others demand of you."

Finally, John thinks, *we're getting to one of the big results I really want.* He wonders how Aaron proposes to pull that miracle off.

"I think the first thing you need to do is find out how to create more time so you can focus on the strategic issues in the company," Aaron says. "You need to get yourself out of day-to-day operations. My suggestion is that you think about making Janice your chief operating officer. She has the skills, she knows what the job requires, and I'm pretty sure she wants to do the job."

John likes Janice a lot. He also recognizes that he's underutilizing her. More than a few complications pop in his head, however.

"You'll need to get out of your own way," Aaron says. "This means learning the fine art of real delegation."

"Real delegation?" John asks.

"This is where you have your people do their jobs without you micromanaging them. It's where you have them run their operations without you looking over their shoulders. It's where you really allow your people to do their jobs. Some of your people will rise to the occasion and some may not. Only the future will tell. But, in each situation we'll know what to do."

John's biggest fear, of course, is that Adam will fail miserably. Then he'd have hell to pay at home. Anne would never stand for such a thing.

"With Janice as your COO, you'll also want to know what's happening with her direct reports by talking regularly with her.

"You and she should meet for at least a few minutes every day about how the Big Rock projects are progressing. And every week or two, Janice, Alicia, and Fred each should put together what we call a 5-15 report on his or her Big Rock."

"What's a 5-15 report?"

Aaron explains. "A 5-15 report is simple. It's only about 300 words. It takes no more than fifteen minutes to write and no more than five to read. And it will save you lots of time by turning over to employees much of the work you've been doing.

"A 5-15 report is designed to help you stay on top of what your direct reports are doing. I'm hoping that they also adopt this reporting system with those who report to them. Remember, simple is great and as Gino Wickman says, 'less is more.' I suggest you also write one and go over it with Janice to get her point of view on how you're doing. I think Janice could be a good accountability partner for you, if you let her."

John scratches his head, "Partner?"

"Not a partner in the way you're thinking, but someone at Aardvark who you'll check in with to see how you're doing. This means you're going to have to let Janice tell you when

you break agreements and are not following through with commitments you've made."

Aaron knows overseeing the transformation of his company will require a lot of John—too much for him to keep his fingers in the daily operation of the plant. This is why Janice is so important in the transformation that John urgently wants for his company.

John agrees to make a list of the day-to-day operational tasks he'll give up to make time for strategizing and establishing much-needed systems. His job focus is to focus on the big picture and chart his company's course; he knows that

But he isn't the only one at Aardvark who must make such adjustments. The operational concerns he removes from his plate he'll have to move onto Janice's. And he isn't sure how she'll react to that amount of additional work. The other key players will have to take up additional slack too, and manage their own agreed upon Big Rocks.

"The most important thing you can do today to make your business sustainable," Aaron says, "is to get yourself completely out of operations."

"I spend most of my time in operations," John says. "If I'm on the manufacturing line, I'm manufacturing. If I'm in my bookkeeping department, I'm doing bookkeeping. If I'm working as an engineer, I'm doing engineering work."

"Okay, John, how much of your time are you spending doing this stuff?"

"I don't know—maybe 30%?"

"When you're doing that sort of work, what's it worth per hour?"

"I don't know."

"What do you pay people to do that sort of work?"

"Somewhere between $15 and $50 an hour."

"Okay, if your work is $50 an hour work, how successful can your company be?"

"I guess it can't be very successful, can it?"

"What do you think?"

"It can't be very successful."

"You're spending 30% of your time doing that kind of work. That means your company is probably much less valuable than it should be."

John takes the information in and frowns.

"I want you to think about your job in terms of the possible roles that you could play," Aaron says.

"There are four roles you can play. You can be a player, a coach, the general manager or the owner. The cool thing about owning a business is you get to choose which of those roles you want to play and how you're going to do it. By the way, the work you just described is what I call player work. These are the things that people do in your company to provide the products you make."

John thinks for a moment and says, "What does the coach do?"

"What do you think a coach does?"

"I don't know."

Aaron knows he needs to move things along. Instead of asking another question he decides to give John the answer. "The coach in the business setting would be a supervisor. Your first-line supervisors are like the assistant coaches. Then you might have your plant manager, who would be the head coach. They're all coaches, nonetheless. They're really just coaching each of the players on how to get the work done in an efficient and effective manner.

"General managers are more strategic. They're actually thinking about 'How do we put the team together? What are the right pieces to have in the right places? Who do we need to draft and who do we need to recruit and who do we need to trade for?'

"Then finally, you have the owners, who have only two jobs: putting a product in the market place that your customers are interested in paying money to buy and hitting the financial goals you require for success.

"But, John, let me ask you a question. If you're a player, how much of your time is going to be spent on tactical day-to-day activities?"

The question hits John in the gut. He's been taking precious time away from big picture tasks, doing things others can do for pennies. He shakes his head.

"John, I think the role you need to take on is one of the general manager and owner. You need to be out of the player and coaching business.

"Let's get out of theory and talk about your company. Your players are your front-line workers. The coaches are your supervisors—Alicia, perhaps, or Fred, or Adam, and most importantly Janice. The general manager would be you.

"How much of your time do you spend as a coach, John?"

"I spend about 30% of my time as a player, so I'm going to say I'm a coach close to 60% of the time."

"So, 90% of your time, John, is spent with day-to-day operational stuff that doesn't add significant value to your company. Does that make sense to you?"

"No."

"If you're the general manger of your company and you acted like the general manager, how much would you be doing in day-to-day operations?"

"Basically little or none. I might talk to a customer once in a while, maybe get involved in some innovation projects, maybe supervise Janice, but probably not much more than that."

"And what would that be worth?"

"That's probably worth about $250 to $500 an hour."

"Okay, if you were to stop being the general manager and only be the owner, what would you be doing?"

"I'd talk to customers and make sure we're doing what we promise and make sure our customers are happy with our products and service. I'd be making sure my financial security value is taken care of properly, which means I would be pricing properly and going after the right customers. But heck, those are both strategic activities. Those aren't things I need to be involved in directly, those are things I could be involved in at some other time down the road."

John pauses to think. He can see lots of obstacles before him. "I'll need to have some system to make sure that those who are working as coaches are doing what they're supposed to be doing. My problem is I don't see how I can accomplish both financial security and keeping our customers happy."

"We'll be putting together a scorecard that's going to help you track the numbers that move the needle in your company. That's going to be Fred's Big Rock. We talked yesterday about Fred putting together key performance indicators that will show what's happening in the company. That will help you know whether your company is on track or off track.

"Let's get back to working on high-value activities. Think about it. If you come up with a new strategy for how to attract the right customer to your company, what would that be worth?"

"Heck, that might be worth a couple of million dollars a year."

"Okay, and how long will it take you to do that?"

John considers the question for a moment. "I don't know, maybe 100 hours."

"Are you telling me that there's work that you can do here that's worth approximately $10,000 per hour, and you're spending your time screwing widgets on your products?"

"When you put it that way, I guess it's kind of dumb, isn't it?" John would laugh at himself if he weren't so shocked.

"Dumb and not knowing are two different things. We'll just call it not knowing; how's that? Here's the goal. I want you to be thinking about how you spend your time, so it can be a $5,000-an-hour activity. If we can find a way to help you work on only $5,000-an-hour activities, what's that going to do for your profits and your company?"

"It'll definitely help it."

"And what will that do for your value of financial security?"

"Definitely help it."

"Do you think we have a pretty good reason, John, for going forward and helping you focus on the $5,000-per-hour job?"

"Yes, but you need to find time for me to do that."

"That's what our next meeting is going to be all about: how we're going to help you become operationally irrelevant."

CHAPTER 10: **DINNER FOR THREE**

Aaron flies in for his next work sessions at Aardvark Manufacturing.

John and his wife, Anne, pick him up at the airport. "I thought it would be a good idea for the three of us to go out to dinner," John says.

Aaron gets in the back of the car, raises a curious eyebrow, and introduces himself to Anne.

After some small talk, Aaron starts asking Anne questions about her involvement in the business and how she feels about what's going on.

She doesn't answer his question directly. Instead she asks, "What are the changes we need to make? I mean, so far, you haven't talked with John about anything that's going to make the company more money."

"Really?" Aaron says. "If the people in the company know what the company is about, and they know what the values of the company are, and John is able to integrate his values into the company, and he's able to change how he spends his time so he's not working on stupid little things that pay $25 an hour, and we get him to focus on things that pay $5,000 an hour or higher, do you think that might have a positive effect on the profitability of the company?"

"I don't know. I don't work there."

Aaron can tell that Anne is no shrinking violet. "Have you ever worked outside the home?" Aaron asks.

"Of course, I have."

"When you worked, where did you work?"

"I worked at the insurance company that's in town."

"What'd you do there?"

"I was an administrative assistant."

"Were you aware of what your boss wanted all the time? Did your boss talk to you about what's important for him, or how you like to communicate with him, or what would make you successful?"

Ann paused to think. Her body language changed from being aggressive to one of being a little confused. "No, I figured it out."

"Okay, Ann, when you were trying to figure it out, how effective were you at your job?"

"Not very."

Listening to the conversation, John thinks, *This is not going to end well. I don't like where this is going.* But instead of speaking up, he decides to keep his mouth shut. And he's glad he does. Because from the conversation, he starts to learn something about his own communication style. He notices Aaron is talking with Anne by asking questions, drawing her out, and he realizes that this isn't how he works with people, particularly his wife.

"You know, I've been listening to you guys talk," John says as they're walking into the restaurant, "and I realize I've made it really hard for people to figure out how to be successful with me because I've never been clear about communicating what success means to me."

"Anne, I've got to tell you," John says, lingering at the reception desk. "Even though we haven't worked on on-time delivery or how to get more sales or how we're going to create cash, all this other stuff is going to make us a way better company. If I actually become clear in my communication we're going to end up having a company where people are going to be much more efficient because they're not going to have to be spending tons of time tying to figure what they need to do. They're going to know what they have to do."

Aaron looks at John and thinks, *I might be getting someplace here. We've been having all these conversations and I*

was wondering whether I was just flapping my gums. Gee, it seems like stuff is sinking in.

As they sit down at the appointed table, Aaron says, "Anne, tell me something. How did you feel when your boss didn't tell you what he wanted or how he wanted it, and you had to figure it out? And when you did something wrong, what happened?"

Anne, seemed to shrink and get smaller after Aaron asked this question. "He would yell at me," Anne says. "Isn't that what all bosses do?"

Aaron says, "I've got to tell you something. I used to do that, and I can only tell you one thing. People hated me. This all began to change when I started asking people questions, and started allowing them to be confident and responsible for what they were doing. And the real change happened when I allowed mistakes to happen."

"Wait a minute," Anne says, holding her hand up. "Now stop right there. What's this mistake stuff? We can't have mistakes. Every time we have mistakes, it costs us money."

"I used to feel that way too. That was until I figured out that there are two types of mistakes, proportional and non-proportional," Aaron says. "A proportional mistake is a relatively small, relatively harmless one—a mistake from which lessons can be learned. A non-proportional mistake is running an airplane into a mountain. There's a big difference, but we tend to lump all mistakes together, to think of them all as bad even though most hold valuable lessons for us."

"I don't know about that," Anne says, folding her arms across her chest.

By now they've opened their menus. They ignore the hovering waiter, put off ordering in favor of concentrating on the deep conversation.

"When you were yelled at, how did you feel?" Aaron says to Anne.

"I didn't like it."

"What did you want to do about it?"

"I wanted to do anything to get back at my boss and I never knew what to do to be successful, and I kept spending a lot of time trying to figure out what my boss actually wanted. When I got it wrong, he would yell at me again. It seemed like a cycle that all employees put up with. Now that you ask, I would have been much more effective if he'd had a better way of teaching."

Aaron smiles. "I'm going to tell you a story I know you'll appreciate. When I was 24, I went to work for my father. If anybody understands family-run businesses, it's me." Aaron could see he had both Anne's and John's attention. "We lasted together for about two months before I ended up going up to a place about 200 miles away. There was one operation my father wanted me to close. Instead of closing it, I expanded it. He said, 'I don't want to go up there anymore. Why don't you buy it from me?' That was great. But it was also terrible. Because from age 24 to 27, the worst possible thing that can happen to a young business person happened to me."

"Oh?" Anne says. "What was that?"

"I was really successful."

"But isn't that a good thing?" John asks.

"When you get somebody who's young and really successful, they feel like they've become master of the universe. I actually thought that all my success was 100% because of what I was doing and had nothing to do with the situation I was in or the people I was working with. Do you know what happens when you have lots of success and you don't really quite understand what brought that success is about?"

"No, what?"

"Your luck finally runs out. Mine did. Instead of everything going my way, it seemed that everything started going against me. I ran out of cash. I had a major embezzlement. I had a serious accident happen in the company. And we bought another company and overpaid by 400%. These

things would have been bad enough. But there was a branch manager in the company we bought who was totally incompetent and I thought he was doing his best to drive the business into the ground.

"It all went south on me because I didn't know what I was doing, even though I thought I did. And when things started going south, I wasn't very good about it. I didn't ask other people questions. I didn't really care. It was obviously their fault, that's what I thought."

John and Anne exchange horrified looks.

"So what did I do? I sat and I yelled at people. I told them they were idiots. Not unlike your boss, Anne, I wanted everything to be run by me. The fact was, when people made mistakes, instead of running them by me, they hid the mistakes from me, and I had to find them myself. When I found them, I went ballistic and called them all sorts of names. So, to deflect blame from them, the people who worked for me either blamed others or tried justifying the behavior that led to the mistake.

"My wake-up call in this whole situation came when I walked into my office one day and started getting these phone calls. They were from suppliers. My suppliers wanted to know when they were getting paid. I couldn't understand why I was getting these calls. I went to my controller and said, 'What's up with this? Why aren't we paying these guys?' He said, 'We are paying them.'

"Around that time, I had a meeting with my CPAs. They said, 'You have a problem.'

"I said, 'What do you mean, I have a problem?'

"They told me I'd lost $250,000 that year. I was incredulous. 'I lost $250,000 this year!? How did that happen?'

"They said they didn't know.

"'How long have you guys known about this?' I asked them.

"'Three months,' one of them told me.

"'Three months? You knew about this for three months and you're only telling me now? Why is that?'

"'Your statements had to be reviewed,' he said.

I didn't have a system in place to make sure our bills were being paid properly. In fact, I wasn't even signing my checks. I was having my controller sign them, because that's what I thought business owners did. The fact was, I wasn't paying attention to our finances, although I thought I was. I thought we were making lots of money. That's what our financial statements said. But my controller had stolen several hundred thousand dollars from me."

John's mouth drops open.

"It was really pretty simple why he stole it. He thought I was a complete jerk. I could use stronger language, but we'll just stay with jerk. He said it was okay to steal from me because I was such a jerk to work for. That started me down the road toward thinking I'd better start doing something differently. If I don't, I probably won't be around for long. But I didn't think that right away. Rather, I thought, what can I do to kill this guy?

"But I just fired him instead.

"That was where I started. That caused me seven years of real problems, because when you lose $250,000 and you have a small company, you don't bail out of that in one year. It took seven years to bail out. It took me negotiating and renegotiating with every supplier I had. I learned a lot during that period. But it was more survival learning than good learning. Once I got past the survival learning, I then started asking myself questions. How can we make this better? Over the last 35 years, I've spent a lot of time asking this very simple question: What makes a sustainable business? When I didn't know what the answer was, I would go and learn something about it.

"That's what we're trying to work on, Anne. If everybody's clear about the values of the company and John is

clear about his values and what he wants his people to do and he lets them go and do it, what do you think might happen?"

"I don't know what to say," Anne says. She takes a moment to formulate an answer. "I guess that might be part of what John needs to do, this thing he keeps telling me he needs to do. I certainly wouldn't want the employees mad enough to seek that kind of revenge."

"And, what might that be," Aaron asks. "These things John says he wants to do?"

"He keeps talking about this thing he calls operational irrelevance. To me this just sounds like giving up and letting his people run all over him."

"Anne, let me ask you something. I've heard from John that you keep talking about wanting to take a two-week vacation. Is that true?"

With that question, Anne's face gets red and she starts to get angry. She seems to think better of it and just answers the question. "It's never going to happen. I just hope it will."

"Do you think that if John actually starts letting his people make decisions based on clear outlines, he'll end up being less involved in the day-to-day operations of the business?"

Anne pauses, looks away. "I guess that could happen. Although it's clear he'll need to keep a finger on the pulse, unless he wants to risk being taken advantage of. Look what happened to you."

"For sure. And we'll talk about that. But, if he's less involved in the day-to-day operations, do you think there's a chance he could actually get away for more than a few days?"

Anne looks slightly hopeful. "I guess that might happen, but I'm not getting my hopes up."

"That's the goal," Aaron says. "John has heard you loud and clear that you want to take more time off with him. Becoming operationally irrelevant is the key to getting that

time, then he doesn't have to be at the center of every decision in the company."

Aaron then goes on to explain what he means. "Operational irrelevance is the goal, but to get there John has to master the art of delegation. We've talked about being clear about what he wants, and allowing mistakes so his employees can learn from them, but we've yet to talk about one really big thing."

"What's that?" Anne asks.

John is curious what Aaron will say.

"The final piece of being able to become operationally irrelevant is learning to trust others and having them trust you. And I know that sounds counterintuitive after the story I've told you. When you were working at the insurance company, did you feel your boss trusted you? Did you trust him?"

"Are you kidding? It was impossible to trust someone who yelled at me. And I guess he didn't trust me, otherwise he would have treated me differently."

"That's the challenge that John has. For years, he's shown through his actions that he doesn't trust others. They've repaid that by always telling John what he wants to hear. It's sort of this ritual dance, one that many owners have with the people who work with them. Right now, that's where John is and it's what he most needs to work on."

John pipes up. "You mean I'm as bad as Anne's old boss? Boy, I must not be very much fun to work with or for."

"That's the big piece of becoming operationally irrelevant that I haven't driven home yet. You must have a high amount of trust in your employees and they a high amount of trust in you, trust that you're not going to do something that's going to hurt them personally."

"Okay. I trust my people."

"Really? If you trusted your people, would you be telling them what to do? Would you be micromanaging them?"

John looks around. "No," he says, "probably not."

"Does that show trust?"

"No."

"John, tell me something. Is trust given or earned?"

"I don't give trust."

"Really, I know that. I got that figured out already." Aaron laughs. So does John, in spite of himself. Anne grunts.

"I guess it's earned."

"Okay," Aaron says, "I'm going to give you something that I read. It's from a book called *The Trusted Advisor*. There's something in this book that I think is just brilliant. It's called the Trust Formula. This book is written for financial advisors, but it works with everybody. The Trust Formula, very simply, is reliability, which means you show up on time, you do what you say you're going to do, and you do it when you say you're going to do it, plus intimacy, which means you care about the other person as a person, not just a thing, plus competency, which means you are good at what you do, divided by self-interest, which equals how much trust you've earned.

"Here's how the formula looks: (Reliability + Competence + Intimacy)/Self-Interest = Trust.

"When you find trust going away, John, it's because at least one of these four things is out of whack. Another person is proving to be unreliable, uncaring, incompetent, motivated by self-interest, or some combination of the four. When you see your employees not trusting what you're saying or doing, you need to ask yourself, 'Which of these four things am I falling down on?'

"In the case of your company, what I've noticed over the past six weeks is that the big issue has been reliability. You don't show much intimacy either, but without reliability there is no way in the world you're going to inspire trust in others.

"In the case of your customers, who you're saying are unhappy, they're probably on their way to not trusting you because you say you're going to ship on Monday but you ship two weeks later."

John starts to understand. "But I have a question. If trust starts to go south, how do I get it back again? Is it even possible?"

"It's pretty simple. You look at the Trust Formula—reliability plus intimacy plus competency, divided by self-interest—and you ask yourself which one is out of whack. And then you fix that one. Oh, and there's one more thing. When you lose trust with someone, you have to tell them that you know you've lost trust and let them know what you plan to do to fix the trust issue. You'll be amazed at the positive effect being responsible for your own actions has on others."

The waiter stops by to refill the wine glasses. John glares at him. "Can't you see that we're busy with our conversation?"

The waiter apologizes profusely and scurries away.

After John's outburst, Anne raises her voice. Her eyes widen with disdain. "John! Why were you so rude to the man? He was simply trying to top off our wine glasses! He was only trying to do his job!"

"What do you mean? I-I wasn't rude."

"John," Aaron says, "answer me this."

John rolls his eyes. "Another question."

"If you were the waiter and you were being spoken to that way, what would you want do with the food you were about to serve?"

When John speaks again, his voice is low, his eyes, downcast. "I think I'd find the lousiest piece of meat I could in the refrigerator, drop it on the floor, step on it a few times, then toss it on the plate. Then I'd hand it to the bum."

"Don't you think you should move out of the lousy-piece-of-stomped-on-meat world into the choicest-piece-of-meat world? Wouldn't it be nice if people did their best because they wanted to?"

"Yes, I do."

"What do you need to do for that to happen?"

"More questions." John grunts.

"Look, I eventually learned that if I don't know how to ask good questions, I was not going to be a very good manager. Because the best managers, the best leaders are curious, and they ask questions. They don't yell. They don't feel the need to be rude."

John looks up. "How did you learn to stop screaming at people? You seem to be so calm when you watch all of the chaos going around me and my business."

Aaron laughs. "The truth is, I learned not to scream through a mistake I made. One day, I was walking through my commissary, the place where we made all of the food for our vending machines, and there was a person making the world's worst-looking sandwiches of all time. I walked up to her and said, 'Tanya, what's that you're doing?'

"'I'm making sandwiches,' she said.

"'Hmmm,' I said. 'One of our pillars in the food-service company is that if you won't eat it, don't serve it. Would you eat that, Tanya?'

"She said, 'No.'

"Tanya was studying my shoes intently at this point because she knew she was in big trouble. And she had reason to be skittish. I was a yeller. I berated and belittled people. I'd say things like 'Tanya, that's crap. Start over. Do it right. You know how to do it. If you don't, get the hell out of here.'

"But for whatever reason, I don't know why, I said, 'Why are you making it for our customers if you wouldn't eat it?'

"She said, 'You made me.'

"I said, 'I did? I just walked in. How did I make you?'

"Tanya looked over at the commissary manager and said, 'She made me.'

"'But she's over working on a different sandwich. How did she make you?'

"We went around circles for this for a while. I kept saying why. Of course, I would've been better off saying, 'What prevented you from doing this right?' But I said, 'Why did you to do this?' And she finally stopped studying my shoes, looked up, put her shoulders back and said, 'I guess it was my responsibility.'

"I said, 'Okay, Tanya, what are you going to do?'

"She said, 'I guess I'll have to start over and redo them.'

"And I said, 'That sounds like a good idea to me.' And I turned around and walked out.

"The real lesson I learned didn't become apparent for several years. My mistake happened to turn out to be a good thing. I learned that asking and not telling got me a lot farther toward helping our people be the best they could be. But it wasn't something that came quickly or easily. I found myself slipping back from time to time, and I had learned that when things weren't going well I needed to start asking myself questions about what I could do differently rather than blaming people who work for me.

"John, this is something I would like to see you do. I would like to see you be able to calmly ask: 'What's different? What we could do differently to get a different result.' Does this make sense to you, John?"

"John," Anne says, "you know the answer to this. We've been talking about it all night."

A dark cloud seems to move across John's face. "I don't get it. I'm the one paying the bill here. I'm the one doing the work. And all you two are doing is finding fault with me."

"It sounds to me like you're feeling attacked," says Aaron

"I do indeed."

"John, which of your values did you just break?"

John furrows his brow, takes a big breath and pauses for what seems like forever. "It sure wasn't financial responsibility." Another pause. "It could be rights and respect."

Aaron smiles to himself but he's not ready to let John off the hook just yet.

Aaron bears down on John. "What about personal responsibility. What, precisely, where you just doing?"

John's face flickers with recognition. "Blaming and justifying," he says.

"Great. Do you want to do anything about that?"

"I don't know what I'm going to do about it. I've been doing this stuff for years and years and years. Can I really change?"

"Look, John, Rome wasn't built in a day. You're going to take one step forward and two steps back, and then two steps forward and one step back. But as you go through this journey, you're going to find over time that you make real progress. That takes commitment and honesty, and if you want to change, I can promise you you'll get better. It's also the only way that you're going to get to operational irrelevance. You can't be lashing out at people, then justifying your actions."

Anne brings up another issue, one that apparently has been on her agenda. "Okay. All of this is well and good. But we have another problem. Quite frankly, I think it's related."

"Okay, Anne," Aaron says. "What's the problem?"

"The problem is our son. You want John to fire him."

Aaron raises an eyebrow. "Let me ask you a question," he says. "Do you know about what's going on at the company, the issue with late deliveries?"

Anne nods.

"And do you know what's going on at the company, the issue with machines breaking down that shouldn't be breaking down?"

Another nod.

"And you know that John has had lots of conversations with Adam about these issues."

Anne sighs.

"You also know, I assume, that Adam's reaction to these conversations is to shout and pout."

She looks down.

"Do you really think that's a good thing to have in the company?"

Anne pauses before she speaks. "No, I don't think that's a good thing to have in the company at all. But hear me, I'm not willing to have my son thrown out into the streets."

Aaron looks at Anne, a mother bear in cub protection mode. "That's a good point," he says. "What would you recommend?"

"I don't know. You're the expert." Anne picks up her menu in a huff.

Aaron decides to ignore the hostility. "Instead of John working directly with Adam, what would you think if Janice became his boss?"

At the mention of Adam working for Janice, John's head snaps around. He's been half listening to the conversation between Aaron and Anne. The mention of his son working for someone else gets hist attention, but he stays silent for the moment.

Anne finally says, "I don't know. I mean, Janice is a much better listener than John. And not nearly as bossy."

"Now wait a minute," John says. "I'm not bossy."

Anne ignores her husband. "It might be worth trying," she tells Aaron. "But no one is firing Adam."

Aaron studies Anne. *This Adam thing could be a real roadblock but if we can get Janice working effectively with him, we might be able to save the kid's job. He does have talent. He's just a pain in the neck.* Aaron decides that fighting this war with Anne right now is the last thing he needs to do.

"Anne, if you really want Adam to stay at the company, we have to consider a few things. First, we never want to kill the goose."

"Kill the goose?"

"Yes, kill the goose. That means above all else, we need to make sure we don't do anything that's going to hurt the company. If that means Adam has to go, then it's for the best. You'd agree that having the company go under would not serve Adam in the long run. If Adam is willing to take responsibility for his actions and commits to doing the things that are necessary to change, then we can have him be on probation, just like we would do with any Aardvark employee who is having problems. That means Adam is likely going to have to take some classes on how to be effective in the company without destroying it."

Anne looks defensive, then seemingly thinks better of Aaron's comment. "I can try to have a talk with Adam about changes he'll need to make. I know he's not going to hear anything that comes out of John's mouth. And, we can try having Janice take over as his direct boss. But, John's still not going to fire him!"

Ah, a tiny bit of progress, Aaron thinks.

Tomorrow's going to be an interesting day, John thinks.

CHAPTER 11: THE BREAKFAST OF CHAMPIONS

T he next morning, John and Aaron meet over breakfast at a diner.

John looks up, smiles at the approaching waiter, and says, "How are you today?"

"I'm great, thank you," the waiter responds. "And you?"

"Couldn't be better. Thanks," John says.

The waiter takes their orders and trots away toward the kitchen.

"What's with you?" Aaron says.

"What do you mean?"

"You just did something you didn't do last night. What was it?"

"I don't know."

"What did we just do?"

"We ordered food."

"And?"

"Oh, I see. I paid some attention to the waiter. I wasn't rude. I even asked him how he was. And I thanked him for taking our order." John pauses for a moment, then grins. "I like this interaction better," he says. "So, what are we talking about today?"

"You need to become operationally irrelevant," Aaron says. "You need to have specific things that you do to make sure you're not involved in the day-to-day operations of your business."

John likes the sound of that.

"Here are the things we need to talk about, and here's our agenda. We'll circle back and talk about each one of these at length.

"One, you need to learn to tolerate mistakes. In fact, you need to make them part of the culture of your company. Every great company handles mistakes well.

"Two, every great leader delegates. You have to realize there's a difference between delegation and abdication. When I say delegate, I mean that over a period of time—not all at once—you're going to assign to others all the work that revolves around day-to-day operations, much of the stuff that you're now doing. And you're going to have a methodology for making sure your delegation is handled properly. That's where EIA comes in."

John has a confused look, "EIA, what's that?"

"EIA is very simple. It stands for expect, inspect, accept. First, you set clear expectations of what you expect, that's the delegation part. Next, you inspect the work that you delegated, this is to make sure it's been done properly. Finally, you accept the work that was done. The real challenge in EIA is the inspect part. It's the step that too many people learning to delegate don't do, and when that happens delegation becomes abdication.

"John, let's take EIA and look at what you do. When you delegate to somebody, what are you doing?"

"I'm setting an expectation for what they're going to do."

"Once they walk out the door after your delegation, do you think they're going to do the job right?"

"If the past is any indication of the future, the answer is no. Which is why I always have to stay in control."

"Ah. Not true. Let me ask you another question."

"Oh, boy, here we go with more questions. Don't you ever do anything besides ask questions?"

"No," Aaron says. "Why do you ask?"

John can't help but smile. "Okay," he says. "We won't play that game. You win." Then he says, "When I told people to do things before, what have I done? Nothing. I don't seem to ever follow up. I just expect them to do it."

"That is the problem, John. When you delegate without inspecting, you've abdicated."

"What do you mean?"

"Let's think about this for a second. Suppose I'm the boss and I've told you I want you to do something. You walk outside my office. You may understand what I said. Or, more likely, you didn't understand it because you don't ask the boss questions, because he doesn't do well with that."

"I answer my people's questions," John says. Once again, he feels defensive.

"Of course, it takes a little bit of effort. And your employees know that if you're pushed, you yell, and they're afraid of getting fired. If you want to delegate, you have to make sure you inspect, and then you have to make sure that you accept the work so the person doing it knows it's been done properly. After all, what did Anne say last night was the most frustrating thing for her when she was working at the insurance company?"

"She never knew if she did the job right."

"How many of the people who work for you are probably in the same situation?"

John looks bewildered and a little bit upset. "Probably way too many."

"Here's the key," Aaron says. "Delegation has to come with inspection and acceptance. Without those steps all you've done is abdicated, which is why you feel like you need to control everything. Your experience is that everything eventually ends up in your lap. Do you think there's a reason for that?"

John says, "I guess that's because I have this fantasy that after I tell someone what to do, they'll just run out and do it correctly the first time. No wonder I have so many problems around here. I'm going to start doing it differently today!"

The waiter arrives with their order. John moves his coffee cup aside to make room for their breakfast. The waiter sets the steaming plates before them, then leaves.

"We're not done yet, John. We've got some other stuff to talk about before you run out and become the new you. We've got to figure out a way of getting all that stuff in your head out of your head and down on a piece of paper. It's easier for your people to do a job the way you'd like them to when they can read a clear description of how it should be done. If there's one thing we've learned, it's that you hate documenting your systems. You have no patience for it. You don't like it. And, frankly, that's one of the reasons your company is sort of stuck at the size it is. You don't have systems for developing excellence, for working through a task in a very specific way. And, that lack of systems starts with you.

"The first thing you're going to need to do—and this is your homework between now and the next time we get together—is you're going to have to write down on a piece of paper all the activities that you will delegate to others, and then you have to choose one of these items to begin with. We'll take these tasks one at a time. The way I'm going to recommend that you do this is to have the person to whom you delegate a task actually document what they're doing. Then you two will get together and you'll review what they're documenting to make sure it's right. This is a great way to help the people you delegate to quickly and deeply understand what they're supposed to be doing."

"Oh, I like that. I don't have to do it. I just have to inspect it."

"That's what delegation is all about."

"Okay, I get the delegation thing. I get that I've got to inspect. I get all that. But what's this stuff about mistakes? You know I hate mistakes and we just can't afford to have them around here. I know we talked about mistakes last night, but I still can't get over the way I feel."

"John, do you make mistakes?"

"Sure, but that doesn't make them okay."

Aaron lifts a piece of toast from his plate. "John, here's another one of my silly statements. Mistakes are the breakfast of champions." He takes a bite and smiles.

"Huh?"

"Remember, no one learns anything new until they make a mistake. It's how we learn everything. Did you ever do something right the first time, unless you were just plain lucky?"

John scratches his chin and thinks for a few seconds. "I guess when you put it that way, I would have to say the answer is no."

"Let's take our conversation about mistakes to a 10,000-foot view and a 20,000-foot view." Aaron raises his toast higher and higher. "As I said before, there are two types of mistakes. There are the mistakes you can afford to make. And there are mistakes you can't afford to make."

"Our customers won't tolerate mistakes at all," John says. He crosses his arms.

"You know that's not true," Aaron says.

John bristles. "What do you mean?"

"What about all this on-time delivery stuff I've heard about for the last six weeks? Has it gotten any better?"

"No." John really is thinking that it's Adam's fault. Instead of acting out which is his usual behavior, he decides to just stay with the conversation.

"What's causing this lack of on-time delivery?"

"There are just too many darn mistakes being made."

"Okay. Have your customers all left you?"

John feels the familiar surge of anxiety. "Not yet, but I'm waiting for them to." He takes another big sip of coffee.

"We're still making the same mistakes and you still have customers. Don't you think there's at least some patience from your customers while they wait for you to get your act together?"

John scowls. Aaron has a point. He waits for him to continue.

"Now, the truth is, if you continue to have poor on-time delivery, eventually your customers will pack up and leave. That's why you want your people to learn from their mistakes and not hide their mistakes from you."

John knows that the mistakes he's aware of are only the tip of the iceberg. He blanches at the thought.

"Let me ask you something, John. When you make a mistake, do you ever make that very same mistake again?"

John searches his memory banks. "Sometimes. But every once in a while I make a mistake only once."

"Okay, good. Let's talk about the times that you made a mistake when you didn't make it again. What happened in between? Was there a question you asked yourself, or was there something you did?"

John picks up his fork and mindlessly cleans it with his napkin. "I would look at what caused the mistake, and then I would change what I was doing so it wouldn't happen again."

"What you're saying, John, is that you probably learned something when you made a mistake."

"Of course. But it wasn't any fun." He dives into his scrambled eggs.

"I bet it wasn't. Some people don't let their ego get involved in mistakes and for others, likely you, mistakes are a hit to your ego."

John isn't sure how to take the comment.

"My wish for you is to have you start looking at mistakes as part of life, to always ask yourself, 'What did I learn?' instead of beating yourself up. Do you remember back when you were a little kid and you were learning to ride a bike?"

"I do, so what?"

"I bet that when you first started riding your bike, you fell off a few times. I also bet that you got back on the bike, made some adjustments, and did a little better the second time Eventually, you learned how to ride a bike and probably got to be pretty good at it. But, and this an important but, you didn't learn it the first time you tried."

"Truth be told," John says, chuckling. "I ended up with a set of stitches before I learned to pop a wheelie."

"For some reason you've lost the ability to adore your mistakes and learn from them. This belief has also infected your entire company. As a result, no one wants to make a mistake and when they do, they do their best to hide it from you and hope you don't stumble across it."

"Adore my mistakes. Now that's funny. Who adores mistakes?"

"I wonder what would happen if you switched things up. I wonder what would happen if, when you found a mistake, you didn't blow a gasket. What do you think would happen if you simply asked your employees, 'What did you learn?'"

John thinks about this for a minute. He can hear the silverware clatter all around him. "I guess they would first wonder what's wrong with me. Then they would either justify why it went wrong, or blame someone else for the mistake. That seems to be how things are done at Aardvark, and it really annoys me."

Aaron thinks back on the first time he tried prying responsible behavior out of his people, how difficult it was. "I can see where this would frustrate you. It certainly would frustrate me. At the same time, is there a possibility that mistakes can be a valuable teaching tool?"

"I guess the answer would be yes if push comes to shove. And, sure, we have to learn that mistakes can be valuable. But, I still don't like it when people make mistakes."

"John, if you make mistakes and you learn from them, what makes you think that the people working for you wouldn't be able to learn from their mistakes as well?"

"I don't know."

"For you to become operationally irrelevant, you need to be aware of the difference between one kind of mistake and another, and you need to integrate that awareness into your business. You and your people have to know what a proportional mistake is and what a non-proportional mistake is. Do you remember we talked about the difference between these two last night?

"Remember last night when Anne was talking about mistakes that cost the company too much money. That's often the response of everyone when I first start talking about mistakes as being gifts. The truth is you need to know the difference between the two types of mistakes."

"Huh?" John stops chewing. He wipes his lips.

"There are two types of mistakes. There's the proportional mistake, which is 99% of all mistakes that will ever happen in your company. Those are the mistakes that happen on a daily basis. Those are the mistakes that you use as learning experiences and teaching opportunities with your people. Those are the mistakes where you'll be asking, 'What did you learn?'

"Then, there's the type of mistake you can't afford, the non-proportional mistakes. Those are the mistakes that can put you out of business. When you think about it, I bet you would have a really hard time coming up with something in the next ten seconds that would put you out of business."

John thinks for a minute then agrees.

"In my experience, we worry about the non-proportional mistakes and we have this false belief that all mistakes will

put us out of business. And as you just conceded, there just aren't that many of them, and it's highly unlikely any of your people would ever make that type of mistake."

"So, all my worry is a waste?"

"Part of the training you'll provide around mistakes will involve your people asking themselves, 'If it doesn't work out, will it put us out of business?' If the answer is yes, what do they need to do?"

"For one, they pretty damn well better have a conversation with me."

"That's perfectly reasonable. But, what if it's a proportional mistake? What if they look at something and say, 'This may have been done wrong?'"

"Frankly, I want to know about those, too." John can feel his blood pressure rising. Time to lay off the coffee.

Aaron looks at John. "Tell me," he says, "if you want to know about every mistake that's been made here, how are you possibly going to become operationally irrelevant?"

John shrugs. He wants freedom more than anything, but it's awfully difficult to release control.

"We need to give you a new script to use when a mistake happens."

"What do you mean?"

"We both know that mistakes are going to happen, and when one does and you become aware of it, here's what you're going to do from now on: You're going to pretend you're me."

"Pardon me?"

"You're going to pretend you're me. You're going to learn to ask questions. When someone makes a mistake, here's what I want you to say. Are you ready?"

"Wait. Are you telling me to do something, instead of asking me a question? That's a first."

"I would do this with questions, but it might take us the rest of our life to figure it out. So I'm just going to tell you, and then we'll figure out why it's important. Every time there's a mistake around you, you're going to ask one simple question. 'What did we learn?'"

"That's it? That's the secret formula?"

"You heard me. Now the question: If you make a mistake and you ask yourself what have you learned, what are you doing?"

John thinks. "I'm skipping through most of the stuff I do when I make a mistake, which is blaming myself and beating myself up and pretending I didn't make the mistake or blaming somebody else for it. I'm making myself personally responsible." He smiles as he connects the dots.

"Absolutely. If you ask yourself what you learned, what does that do for personal responsibility? How does that make you a better leader? At the end of the day, for your business to grow, you have to move from being a manager to becoming a leader."

"Okay, I get it. I've got to start allowing mistakes." He makes a show of pounding his fist on the table.

"Okay, let's go to your office. I'll accept 'allowing mistakes' for now, but you're going to have to go from allowing them to loving them if you want to grow, if you want your business to grow. Just think that when a mistake happens you've just received a gift and that gift is going to allow your people to learn and grow."

The two exit the diner and walk toward their cars. "There's one more thing," Aaron says. "When you see a mistake, I know your tendency and, for that matter, almost everyone's tendency is to blame the person who made the mistake. In my experience, that's rarely the cause. It's typically a system problem, which is why having great systems is incredibly important. When your people make mistakes, instead of blaming someone, I want you to look at the system.

By doing that, you're going to have a much better chance at permanently fixing the problem. And, of course I want you to ask them what they've learned from the mistake that occurred."

"This next thing is important." Aaron pauses, takes his car keys out of his pocket. He's delighted that John is getting his teaching points, but he doesn't want to drop this ball. "Most of the time, you're going to have to pull teeth to get an answer from an employee. You have a long history of yelling at people when you find a mistake. At first, your people just aren't going to believe that you've changed. It's part of the penance you're going to be paying for being a my-way-or-the-highway sort of guy.

John takes a deep breath. "This is a lot to think about, and it's only 9 a.m." He glances again at his watch.

CHAPTER 12: OPERATIONAL IRRELEVANCE IS THE GOAL

Aaron gets a cup of coffee from one end of the conference room and settles into a seat along one of the table's long sides. John gets coffee and takes his accustomed seat at the head of the table.

Aaron says, as if seeing the place for the first time, "This is a nice conference room, John. It's much nicer than the rest of your plant."

"This is where we meet with customers."

"That's interesting. I wonder how they feel about the rest of the plant when they walk through it. Because things aren't always in the place they should be as I walk around. I have to step around a lot of stuff."

"We can talk with Janice about that."

As if on cue, Janice walks briskly into the room.

From what John has said, Janice previously worked for a major manufacturer with 2,000 employees. An outsider, Aaron thinks, might ask why Janice left her job with the large manufacturer and ended up at Aardvark with all the problems they have.

Janice settles into the seat opposite Aaron.

"Janice," Aaron says, "here's something we're trying to do with John. John's goal over the next year is to become operationally irrelevant. When I say operationally irrelevant, what do you think that means?"

Janice furrows her brow. "I've never even heard that term," she says. "What does it mean?"

"If you were to guess, what would you say it means?"

"Probably that John wouldn't be required to make the company function."

"That's close. And where are we today with John?"

Janice is wary of being honest, Aaron can see this. She's clearly seen that in the past those who are honest with John often get the brunt of his temper.

"If John were to leave, I think we'd have a big problem, because he's really right in the middle of almost everything we do. But I've got to be honest, John, there's also a down side to your involvement in the daily operations. Your being right in the middle of everything sort of creates a bottleneck. At my last job, we really focused on what it would take to get rid of bottlenecks. Maybe we should do that with the late-delivery problem."

"That seems to make sense," Aaron says.

John chimes in, "That seems to make sense to me, too. What do you think we should do, Janice?"

"I'm kind of stumped. We don't have enough people. Most of us are barely getting our jobs done, which may be part of the late-delivery problem."

"We don't have money in the budget to hire anybody else right now," John says. "We have to solve this with what we have."

Aaron says, "Let's take a look. What's the root cause? What's the thing causing you to have bad on-time delivery?"

"We have this finishing machine that we use as the last step in polishing our most difficult parts, and that keeps breaking down," Janice says. "Adam's responsible for keeping it running, but he just keeps telling me it's old and needs to be replaced. I kind of take that to mean Adam really doesn't want to deal with fixing the machine. John, do you have any more information that I don't have?"

"I haven't even talked to Adam about this, because, frankly, I thought you were taking care of it."

"John, remember when we were talking about values?" Aaron says. "One of the values we talked about was personal responsibility. What's going on right now?"

"Janice seems to be blaming me and I seem to be blaming her, is that about right?"

"What do you think?"

Janice watches and listens to this exchange in stunned silence. "John," she eventually says, "are you saying I should take this over and you're going to let me solve the problem?"

"Yep," John says. "That's exactly what we're going to do. This is something we need to fix quickly. We can't have late deliveries."

Janice looks relieved. "Probably the best thing to do is for us to sit down with Adam and for you to tell him in front of me that he's now reporting to me and not to you. That's step one, and I have no idea where that's going to go." She pauses for a moment, seemingly choosing her words carefully. "But you know Adam can be tough. What happens when he runs to you and says I'm making him do stuff we shouldn't be doing?"

"Good question. What do you think we should do?" John asks. He knows how easily he jumps to get involved and doesn't know how he will change his M.O., particularly when it comes to his son.

John and Janice both look at Aaron, who's sitting with his arms crossed. "I'm just watching this," Aaron says. "You guys solve this. I want to see how you do."

John studies Janice as he thinks through the dilemma. "It used to be that I would tell you what to do and you would go do it, or maybe not." Janice acknowledges the assessment by nodding her head. "Let's try something new. What do you think we should do?"

Janice seems surprised; then she leans forward in her seat. "I think we should take a hard look at that machine and see what's happening with it. Maybe we should bring somebody

in to help Adam get it fixed as fast as possible so we can get the products out."

"If that machine is our problem," John says, "then why don't we get it fixed and why haven't we done it yet?"

Janice recoils. Both men pick up on her reaction. Then a determined look plays across her face. "You haven't given me permission to do anything about it. Now that you have, I'll get it fixed. But we need to be thinking about this in a broader manner, John."

"What do you mean?"

"We're always running into various problems, and it seems nothing ever happens to fix them until you get involved. You then tell me what to do to solve the problem and I then have to jump through a zillion hoops to get it done. Sometimes there's enough time, but most of the time there isn't and as a result both Aardvark and I look really bad. And then, there's Adam…"

Aaron pipes up. "Let's think about this in a way that might make some sense. Janice, you're aware of lean manufacturing methods, right? I'm sure you guys used it at your last job. All big companies do."

For John's benefit Aaron explains, "John, lean manufacturing is also known as the Toyota Production System. I don't recommend you adopt what Toyota does, but you do want to take parts of it, especially the concept that you're constantly and always looking for ways to eliminate waste."

"We actually did," she says. "It was a very good process. We had systems and processes that allowed everyone to know what they were supposed to do."

"Is there any process like that here?"

"No. We don't really look at systems and because of that, our quality is often spotty. I mean we've got good quality. Once something gets out the door, it's really good stuff. We have to have systems in place that allow us to have consistent products along the manufacturing process and not just when

it goes out the door. Instead of building quality in, we have a bad habit of inspecting for quality. I can't tell you how expensive this is and how it's one of the root causes for things getting out the door late. For me, again, it comes down to our lack of systems."

"Understood. Now let's step back a moment. What did you mean by a bottleneck when you first mentioned the late-delievery problem?" John asks. He knows what it means, but he'd like her to put words to it.

"I mean the kind of bottleneck you get when a machine, system, or person gets in the way of doing things the way we want them to get done, meaning on time and with great quality. The funny thing about bottlenecks, like our machine that keeps breaking down, is when one gets solved, another jumps out to take its place. What we need is a system for handling bottlenecks as they appear."

Aaron then looks at John and asks, "John, who might be the big bottleneck in this company? At least, most of the time?"

John thinks he sees what Aaron is doing. He thinks this is a chance for him to be responsible and not blame someone else. It's probably time for him to be honest and admit his mistakes. "Well," he says slowly, "I would have to say I'm probably the bottleneck most of the time."

Aaron says, "Perhaps, but in this particular case, who do you think the bottleneck is?"

"I'd have to say it's Adam." *That's it*, he thinks, *it's Adam*. "The finishing machine's still not fixed. And he hasn't come to me, nor has Janice. So we're just stuck here."

"Is Adam really the bottleneck?" Aaron says. He looks at Janice. "Janice, is Adam the bottleneck here?"

Janice looks around. She appears nervous. Aaron is sure she's reluctant to tell the truth. Based on what he's witnessed, he doesn't blame her.

Janice turns to John. "You know, I actually think that you're the bottleneck. I think you were right the first time." Janice shrinks a little.

John's face gets red. He can feel his temperature rising. Aaron waves a finger at him. John pauses, takes a breath, and counts to three. That's what Aaron told him to do when he's feeling challenged, when he feels the need to defend himself. "You know, I think you're right, Janice," John says. "I probably am the bottleneck. What might be the steps for me to take to get out of the way?"

Janice sets her elbows on the conference table. "The first thing I would like you to do is meet with Adam. You need to tell him I'm his boss. And when Adam comes back to you, which he's sure to do, you can't answer his questions. You have to send him back to me so I can answer them."

"You think you're delegating," Janice continued, "but when people come back to you, you take away all my authority by solving a problem or dealing with an issue that's my responsibility. If you want to get together with Adam and me, that might be okay. But most of the time you're going to have to say, 'Adam, have you talked to Janice about this?' And when Adam says no, you'll need to say, 'Talk to Janice, and if you guys can't work it out, then come back and see me together.'"

John looks at Aaron. "What do you think?"

"That sounds like a reasonable solution to me. Because what are you doing when you send Adam back to Janice?"

"I guess I'm helping Janice keep the authority she needs to do her job. And I'm letting Adam know that he can't do an end run by coming to me."

John feels an inexplicable sense of relief. Maybe he can fix the Adam problem. Maybe he can get away for a couple of weeks with Anne without having the whole world fall apart. Maybe he can spend his time on the tasks that really matter, the ones that add to the bottom line.

"Yes," Aaron says, "that sounds about right to me, and when you don't take Adam's bait, what else are you doing?"

John stares at a picture on the wall and then turns to Aaron. "I think that when I turn Adam back to Janice, it's a step toward becoming operationally irrelevant. Does that make sense?"

Aaron nods his head. He grins. "Now, we're getting someplace."

Janice says to John, "Why don't we ring Adam right now and have a conversation about this machine. And you can specifically give me the authority and the responsibility to supervise Adam and get this machine fixed."

"Sounds like a good idea to me," John says.

"I kind of like this conversation you guys are having," Aaron says. "Is this something that happens around here a lot?"

Janice laughs. "Are you kidding? We've never had a conversation like this here. This is a first. I really hope it continues, because I think it might make our company a whole lot better."

The receptionist sticks her head in the room and signals for John. He gets up and leaves the room.

"I bet you're wondering if John will get out of the way and allow you to do your job," Aaron says the moment John exits. "That's a really good question, one that I hope will be answered with a yes. At the same time, this is going to be a two steps forward and one step backward thing."

Janice looks at Aaron with a puzzled expression. Aaron continues. "You know when you're trying to learn a new skill, it never goes in a positive direction all the time. You always experience regression." Janice nods. "That's what will likely happen with John. I think he realizes what he needs to do. Now, it's going to take you being brave and giving him honest feedback in order for him to become the operationally irrelevant owner we all want to see.

"That means that you're going to have to be the designated manager to help him with that goal. I know it's scary, but here's the reality: John won't be firing you. In fact, I've found that when you get past John's bluster, he's a pretty good listener. You just have to get past the bluster first, and we're going to work on that, also. If John is going to become a great delegator, he's going to need to be a good listener and keep his temper under control. I'm hopeful that he'll be able to do this."

"Me too," Janice says.

"John will need to stick to what he's good at, which is strategic innovation and sales, and let you guys run the business. If he does, this company will become bigger and more successful."

"Sounds good to me."

"We're simply trying to get to a place where you can run the day-to-day operations, and for that to become a reality, we'll have to install a whole bunch of systems. These systems are going to help support you and support John and allow all those who work here to do their jobs in an efficient and effective manner."

"Amen to that."

CHAPTER 13: **THE EFFECTS OF FINANCIAL INSECURITY**

Before their next session, Aaron meets John for dinner. They once again go to the restaurant where they and Anne had eaten a few weeks before. Aaron is starting to think that John is a creature of habit. This might make things a bit difficult when it comes to John making permanent changes in his behavior.

"Let's start tomorrow with a meeting with all of your managers," Aaron says. "Besides continuing our conversation about purpose and your values and mission, we'll announce that Janice will become your COO."

"That's an awful lot of stuff to cover," John says. "Aren't we taking a big risk by doing so many things so quickly?"

"It's time for us to start moving forward," Aaron says. "The planning is over. It's time to start implementing."

"Okay, if you say so. But, frankly, I'm nervous." John starts to fidget which is Aaron's signal that it might be a good idea for him to back off a little and let John get comfortable with what he just talked about.

"Everybody who goes through this sort of thing is nervous. This is a hard thing you're doing. You've been running this company for over 25 years. It's your baby."

"It's actually 28 years but, you're right, it is my baby, and I'm scared about letting go of daily operations. What happens if people start making mistakes and things go wrong and our customers leave and…"

Aaron cuts him off with a raised hand. "John, remember the conversation we had about mistakes?" he says. "What did we talk about?"

John thinks. "We talked about how there are two types of mistakes—those we can't afford and those we learn from."

"I'm guessing you probably learned from both kinds of mistakes. Instead, let's think of them as mistakes that you're willing to have and mistakes that you're not. Remember, we can't see all mistakes as bad. In fact, some mistakes are magnificent because they allow you to learn."

John pictures all the things that could go wrong. Adam blowing up, Janice quitting, the machine breaking down for the thousandth time, Fred missing something big in receivables.

"Let me tell you another story from my days of owning my vending company," Aaron continues. "We had a horrible time hiring, training and keeping route drivers. We would spend six to eight weeks having a trainer ride with them in the field. At the end of that time, we would have them go out on their own. Usually, the first day was horrible. If the driver managed to finish the route in less than 16 hours, it was a miracle. All too often drivers would get frustrated and quit before they really learned what they were doing.

"One day as I was walking through our warehouse, I noticed we had a full bank of machines that were prepped and ready to go into the field. The thing is, we weren't going to need these machines for about four or five weeks. Someone had made a mistake by getting them set up long before they were needed.

"I don't remember who came up with the idea, but we had just hired a new driver and decided to train him on these machines. Without the distractions, we figured we could really teach him how to fill and clean the machines properly.

"Instead of six to eight weeks to get this driver up to speed, we did the training in two weeks. When this new driver started his route, he finished in ten hours and was really happy with what he had done. We then tried the same thing several months later when we hired another driver and, lo and behold, the exact same thing happened. The driver was

ready to go; got done on his first day in ten hours and was equally thrilled.

"This new method of training was a mistake. We had no idea it was going to turn out the way it did. It was only because of this very nice happenstance—having a bank of prepped machines long before I needed them— that I came up with what I call the magnificent mistake. The only way a magnificent mistake can happen is by letting mistakes happen in the first place."

John thought about the last time an employee made a mistake that had turned out to be a good thing. He drew a blank. Was he simply forgetting?

John took a look around the restaurant. He saw lots of mistakes being made, like their waitress forgetting to bring bread and having to be reminded to do so. He thought to himself that there were little mistakes all around him all the time. He just never took time to notice them.

"When your people feel free to experiment, some of them will have unbelievably great results. But, it has to start with a culture of experiments for this to happen."

"But still. It's scary, and I hate doing this."

"I certainly understand this. What's your desired outcome, John?"

"You know what my desired outcome is."

"I do. But why don't you tell me just in case I'm forgetting something."

"When we started this process, I thought I wanted the business to grow and become more profitable. I wanted to be able to take Anne on a vacation, to get away on occasion. I certainly wanted to figure out what to do about Adam. But I realize I want more. I want to be able to retire. I want my kids to be able to take over the business if they're good enough. I want to be able to sell the business if I have to. And, for sure, I want to have a business that's bigger and more successful."

"Why do you want bigger and more successful?"

"Because I can't afford to do all the things I want to do. We don't have money for growth. And, frankly, we're not putting money away for funding growth. We don't have a big safety cushion here. I'm not saving much for retirement."

"Those four reasons are really important. Here's something for you to consider and a question for you to ask. What have you done to prevent those four things you want from happening? How are you bottlenecking the financial health of your company?"

John thinks a moment and then says, "This bottleneck word is starting to annoy me."

CHAPTER 14: FINANCIAL
CHALLENGES ARRIVE

L ater that day, John escorts Aaron to the conference room where he finds Janice; Fred, the controller; and John's daughter, Alicia. Adam has not been included in the meeting because he's not a member of the senior management team. John excuses himself for a moment to take a call, leaving Aaron alone with the team.

Aaron sits at one of the table's long sides toward the end. "Happy to see you again, Janice," he says.

"I'm happy to see we're making progress and getting stuff out the door on time," Janice says. "My working with Adam on our problem seems to have worked out better than I thought it would. The machine's now running 80% of the time, and that's improvement enough for now; we're not shipping stuff late. But neither are we yet where we want to be."

"If you were, what would be different?"

Janice takes a moment to think, tilting her head to one side. "We'd find a way to keep enough parts in stock, and we'd have more people besides Adam trained on how to fix the machine when it goes down."

"Is that part of your plan?"

"It is indeed," Janice says. Aaron notices how commanding she now appears to be. *That's good*, he thinks.

The rest of those present silently listen to Janice and Aaron. From the look on their faces, it's obvious that they're struck by how differently things seem to be working now.

After 20 minutes, John saunters into the meeting, sits down, and addresses the group. "Okay, let's get started," he says.

Aaron looks at him. *This is something we'll need to talk about,* he thinks. *Meetings need to start on time, call waiting or not. They also need to end on time. And they need to be efficient.*

"Okay," John says, "the purpose of this meeting is to make a major announcement. I need to become what Aaron calls operationally irrelevant in this company."

Noticing that almost everyone except for Janice looks confused, Aaron steps in. "John," he says, "why don't we step back for a second and let people know why you need to be operationally irrelevant and, more important, what operational irrelevance is."

John nods. "By operationally irrelevant," he says, "I mean that I no longer will be involved in day-to-day operations. But I say that only as a preface to the announcement I want to make. The main reason I called this meeting is to let everyone know Janice is going to become our chief operating officer."

Janice's eyes fly wide open. "What?" she says.

"Oh," John says. "I forgot to tell you, Janice."

Aaron laughs out loud. Everyone looks at him like he's a loon. "John," he says, "didn't we talk about open communication and letting people know what you're thinking? You just made this major announcement in front of everybody and you haven't even asked Janice whether she wants the job?" Aaron looks at Janice. "Janice, I'm a big fan of having the right person in the right seat. John and I have had conversations about having you in this particular seat. How do you feel about being there?"

John's not used to having others call him out, especially in front of his staff. His impulse is to change the course of the conversation, to shift the focus toward people being respectful of him. But he decides to let it slide this time. John doesn't want to be seen as a whiner, but he's having a difficult time staying neutral.

"John," Janice says, "are you willing to give me the authority to do the job?" She wears a doubtful expression.

John nods.

Aaron locks eyes with John. "I didn't hear what you said, John." His voice is playful and serious at the same time. "Are you willing to give Janice the authority she needs to do the job and not just the responsibility?"

John realizes he's been having a conversation with himself, that he hasn't actually voiced his thoughts. He leans in and addresses Janice, "Yes," he says clearly, slowly. "I'm willing to give you the authority." He hesitates. "Although, there are going to be times where you'll have to remind me what I just said."

"Are you willing to step out of the way and not let people do end-runs around me?" Janice says.

"I'll try."

"Can I step in here for a second?" Aaron says, fishing around in his pocket for a pen. "I have an experiment I want John to do." He gets up, walks over to John, and extends the pen at arm's length. "John," he says, "I want you to try to take this pen out of my hand."

"Huh?"

"I want you to try to take the pen out of my hand." He wiggles the pen.

John puts his hand over the pen but doesn't touch it.

"No, John," Aaron says. "I want you to try to take the pen out of my hand."

"What do you think I'm doing?" John says, annoyed. He's never been a fan of magic tricks or unnecessary interruptions.

"Well, it's a pretty lousy try," Aaron says.

"There's got to be a point here," John says, exasperated and more than a little embarrassed. "Can we get to it and

stop playing games?" He swipes the pen out of Aaron's hand and slaps it on the table.

Aaron says, "When you tried to take the pen out of my hand, you either left the pen in my hand or you took the pen out of my hand. Do you see that?"

John scowls. He doesn't get the point. And there's nothing he hates more than being embarrassed in front of his senior management team.

"Did you learn anything about trying to do something?" Aaron says, ignoring John's annoyance.

"I guess I learned that trying is pretty hard."

"When you tell Janice you're going to try, what are you really saying?"

John finally understands. There's no trying. You either do it or you don't. "Would it be that I'm giving myself an out when I decide to go back to my old behavior; telling people what to do and not really delegating?"

Aaron nods. "So, what happens when you revert back to your old ways? What happens when you sort of try, but not?"

John crosses his arms and sighs. "I guess I'll have to apologize. And work on not allowing the end-run next time it's tried."

"That's right. So, everybody here, what's the lesson we got from this?" Aaron looks from one face to the next.

With the exception of Janice, the members around the table look nervous. Aaron knows that they're reluctant to give the wrong answer because John has always punished the wrong answer.

Aaron breaks the uncomfortable silence. "You know, we have some work to do here regarding how all of you run this company. If Aardvark is going to move forward, you have to stop walking on eggshells and tell John the truth. I thought we established that. As to giving the wrong answer, here's the lesson I want you to learn: You're either successful at doing

something or you're not. And when you're not successful, what do you call that?"

Janice, who has spent far more time with Aaron than the others, pipes up. "When we don't do it, I would consider that a mistake."

"Right. Let's talk about mistakes for a second."

Once again, Aaron brings up the concept of affordable and unaffordable mistakes. "If John comes in and steps over you and takes your authority away, whose mistake is that?"

"That's his mistake," Janice says.

"Is that a mistake we can afford, or is that a mistake we can't afford?" Aaron asks.

"That's a mistake we can afford, as long as it doesn't happen all the time."

"Okay," Aaron says. "And what is your response going to be, Janice?" He gives her a raised eyebrow as a prompt.

Janice pauses to think for a few seconds. "I'm going to need to talk to John, and John's going to need to listen."

"But, how have you talked to John about this sort of thing in the past?"

"I told him that I found it annoying." She shoots John a look out of the corner of her eye. His face betrays no emotion.

"How did John react?"

"He got defensive."

John doesn't like what Janice is saying, but he knows it's true. He sighs, which appears to make Janice nervous.

"Janice," Aaron says, calling her attention back. "Do you think there might be a different way that we could start that conversation with John?"

Janice furrows her brow. She shrugs, no doubt thinking that she's already gone too far.

"What do you think would happen if you started with a question?" Aaron says. He looks at John and says, "John, if Janice asked you a question about the mistake you made instead of telling you she was annoyed, how might you react?"

"It depends on how she says it," John says.

Aaron leans in. "What's the question I've asked you every time we've talked about mistakes, John?"

"I know this one because you've asked it 9,000 times: 'What did I learn?'"

Aaron looks around the room. "What did we learn by this, everyone?" Janice opens her mouth to speak, but Aaron raises a hand. "Janice and John, you can't answer. One of the other folks has to."

Alicia pipes up. "I guess you're kind of forcing us to be responsible for ourselves. You either are successful or not and you need to take responsibility for the result. I guess that would be an example of personal responsibility."

"That's exactly what we're doing," Aaron says. "If I ask you a question, you get to own the issue. If I tell you what to do, who owns the issue?"

"I guess you would, wouldn't you?" Alicia says.

Aaron nods. He thinks that working with Alicia is probably going to be a lot easier than working with her brother. It seems she has the ability to pick up on things quickly. Aaron thinks he'll probe this further, but for now it's time to keep the meeting moving forward.

"Okay, let's get to the reason we're all together right now and that's to talk about some conversations that John and I have been having. We've been discussing how to get him out of the way, but still have enough control over the company to feel comfortable delegating real responsibility and authority to others."

Fred, the controller says, "It'll never work. John's not going to do it. If he hasn't done it in 20 years, what's going to make us believe he's going to do it now?"

This was new for John. It was the first time Fred had challenged him in a very long time. John also feels that this is a good move even though it feels really wrong and hard to listen to.

"That's a really good question," says Aaron. "Let's talk about this for a while. The big problem for John is that, although the company appears to be successful, it's not performing in a way that will allow John to step away and feel comfortable about his financial situation. Because of this, he's felt he's needed to micromanage every aspect of the business.

"The truth is, because of his micromanagement the opposite has happened. John has bought himself a good job, but the company is not in a position to be financially sustainable and allow a next generation to come in and run it."

Right after Aaron says this, Alicia looks like she swallowed a frog. A few seconds later a look of understanding crosses her face.

"If John doesn't make these changes, that's the way the company will die," Aaron continues. "John is committed to having the company become personally and economically sustainable, which means he either gets out of the way of day-to-day activities, or the company keeps stumbling along like it has for the past several years. And stumbling along like always is the best case scenario."

Fred looks at Aaron. "What do you mean it's not financially sustainable?" he says. "I've been here for 20 years, and we've never been out of cash, we've never missed a payment, we've never bounced a check."

"That's true, Fred, and you've done a great job with that," Aaron says. "But, let me ask you a question. You have a 401(k) system here, right?"

"Yup," Fred says.

"How much is John saving in that?"

Fred pulls the figure off the top of his head. "About $7,000 a year."

"Is that enough money for John to retire?" Aaron folds his hands on the table.

"Isn't he going to get money out of the company?"

"Do you think he'll get enough money out of the company to retire?" Aaron raises an inquisitive eyebrow.

"I don't know. It's not my problem."

John starts to wonder whether it's time for Fred to go. First, he insults him with his management style and now he's saying that whether he can retire or not is not his problem. John is learning a hard lesson. His employees don't really care about John's success. They care about their problems and issues.

Aaron continues, "That's one issue. Do you have an emergency fund in case business goes bad for a period of time?"

"We have about $100,000."

"Is that enough? If something goes wrong, say you lose a customer like XY, will that cover the company?"

"Not in my book. I'd like to have to have six months' expenses put aside."

"How much would that be?"

Fred looks up in the air. "About $600,000."

"Sounds like there's a pretty good gap there. Let me ask you another question. If you guys had a chance for growth, where would the money come from?" This time Aaron looks to John for the answer.

John says, "I haven't had to worry about that for a while."

"Do you think you might have to worry about that?"

"I don't know. I guess so."

John leans back in his chair and thinks for a second. Aaron decides to let a bit of silence take over the room while John thinks about growth. John turns his attention back to Aaron and Aaron continues.

"Let's pause and talk about that for a moment. If you were to grow the company by 50%, if you were to become a $9 million company, what's that going to cost you?"

"I don't know. How would I know that?"

"Why don't you just take a guess?"

"Maybe $800,000."

"Where might that money come from?"

"We'd borrow from the bank."

"Do you think the bank will loan you all the money you need?"

John frowns. "Probably not. And we don't have money for that, either. The interest payments alone would kill us."

"Let me ask you again, Fred. Is the company making enough money?" Aaron looks at the comtroller.

"When you put it like that, I guess it isn't."

Aaron continues. "That's one of the things John and I will have to talk about. You need to have enough money, which means you need to grow the business. You need to grow the profits. You need to get better at what you're doing. And you've had too many things getting in the way of doing so. Guess what's been getting in the way the most?"

Fred looks at Aaron. "Are you kidding? If I answer that question honestly, I'll be fired!"

"You're not going to get fired," Aaron says. "And I do want you to answer honestly. Tell me what you think."

John pipes up, "Fred, if I haven't fired you by now, then it's not going to happen today."

Fred leans back and falls silent. He looks disinclined to take Aaron at his word.

Alicia breaks the silence. "I know the answer to this," she says.

"Okay," Aaron says, turning his gaze toward John's daughter. "What is it?"

"It's got to be my dad. He's the one who gets in the way."

The room fills with laughter while John's face goes red.

Aaron turns to John. "What do you think?"

John takes a long time to answer. He draws a big breath. He knows that the people in the room are waiting for an explosion. That's what always happens when he's pushed. "It's true. Like we discussed, I am in the way, and I need to get out of the way." There's no denying the truth. He sees the situation he's created in black and white.

CHAPTER 15: **LIVING WITH THE MISSION STATEMENT**

L ater, John, Janice, and Aaron head out to lunch. They go to the very same restaurant that John and Aaron went to the first time Aaron came out to visit. They even have the same waitress. She not only recognizes John, who's a regular, but also Aaron.

Aaron is impressed. He says so to no one in particular. "If more businesses had employees like our waitress, I think the level of service in the U.S. would be much better than it is today. Way too many businesses consider their customers an inconvenience. The fact is, at least for me, customers are the reason a business exists. It would be really nice if more businesses acted that way."

Janice looks thoughtful. "I see what you mean. It's got me thinking about our mission statement, 'We make our customers' lives easier.'"

They'd spent an hour talking about Aardvark's mission statement during the meeting. Everyone agreed that doing a job well and creating satisfied customers would end up making the company profitable. Chasing money for the sake of money would not.

"When I'm talking to people," Janice continues, "I think it would be smart to ask myself, 'Is this helping make our customers' lives easier?' And if it's not, then we probably need to be doing something differently. That's especially true in engineering."

"You've got it," Aaron says. "What you want to do is make sure the mission statement is integrated into everything you do." Aaron turns to John. "Every time you have a meeting; and, Janice, every time you have a meeting, what do you need to do at the outset?"

Janice leans forward, but looks confused.

John shrugs.

"Okay, I'll answer this for you," Aaron says. "You start every meeting you have with the statement, 'We make our customers' lives easier.' Then you need to ask the question, 'What have we done toward that end this week? What could we do differently to make our customers' lives easier?' If you do these things, what might happen at Aardvark?"

Janice answers. "John wants the company to be financially secure, and he wants to have the ability to take a few weeks of vacation with Anne without worrying about losing a major customer like XY and the company going under. He hasn't forgotten any of that. He wants to be able to retire and to eventually turn the business over to his children, at least Alicia. And now that I've agreed to manage Adam, he expects that problem to diminish or to resolve itself without him having to fire his son. If everyone gets on the same page by buying into the mission, he'll be that much closer to his goals."

John pipes up. "It's really one of the things we need to do if we want me to get out of the way because I need to know that we're working on stuff that is useful and makes our customers' lives easier. Here's why: If we aren't successful with this, then I won't be able to retire. I won't be able to let go. I won't be able to back off."

Aaron leans back. It's clear that both John and Janice understand the importance of the mission. Without it, there's no cohesion, no getting John free.

They all study their menus. When the waitress comes back, they place their orders. Once the drinks are delivered, they get down to business.

"Janice," Aaron says, "let's talk about your role as COO. We weren't really fair to you at the meeting today. We just sprung this on you without getting your permission and having a full conversation about what it means."

"I'm glad we're having this discussion, because, frankly, I was a little upset that you didn't talk with me before announcing it to everyone." Janice appears to be choosing her words carefully.

John is surprised. Who would resent a promotion? Then he thinks twice. He runs a tight ship. People don't always like additional work dropped in their laps, which is what happens often enough. "Janice," he says, "you should know that with more responsibility, you'll get a raise. I'm not asking you to take on more without getting paid for it."

"Thanks, John," she says. "I'm glad you're doing that. But it's not what I was concerned about. I'm really concerned that I'm going to have Alicia and Adam reporting to me. I feel like I'll be babysitting your kids." She clears her throat.

Aaron notices Janice's nervous posture. *She's got guts*, he thinks. "You know, Janice, I can understand why you may see it that way, because, in a way, you are. What's likely to happen is that, as Alicia learns to do her job properly, you'll be able to move her around the company so she learns how to do all the management jobs. Because someday, she might be in a position to take over for her dad. When that happens, she'll go from reporting to you to being your boss. I call what you're about to do not babysitting but being a leapfrog manager.

"In other words, you're playing a really important role. You're going to be the chief operating officer of the company and whether Alicia works for you or you for her, you're still going to have the same job. My main concern is that her MBA could get in the way of learning the practical aspects of running a business. Too often, newly minted MBAs are so theoretical that they never learn what it takes to make a smaller business run. That's where you come in. You'll make for a wonderful teacher because you understand the day-to-day of this organization. As we all know, Aardvark doesn't

have the resources of a big business. And this is a lesson Alicia will have to learn."

Janice runs her finger along the edge of the menu. She seems to be considering Aaron's statement very carefully. "I need to learn some stuff, too, if I'm going to help Alicia because, frankly, I know a lot about operations, but I don't know anything about sales, the way Stan does. I don't know much about finance, the way Fred does, either. I'm feeling a little like a fish out of water here, and that's something I really don't like feeling."

Aaron asks, "If you want to learn these things, Janice, what might you do?"

"Obviously, I would take some classes. And I might have some help come in to tutor me. I've never been responsible for sales and marketing but have always found it interesting. I do know that my knowledge is limited in those areas and getting outside help is probably going to be necessary for me to an effective leader in this part of the business."

"John," Aaron says, "it sounds to me like we might need some help in marketing and sales. Along with Janice learning from others, I would love to work with her on creating a sales and marketing system that works.

"I have a great system. One that's proven and will do the job, Mind you, it'll take some time to implement. We might even want to have Janice and Alicia attend the program where I learned it. The system was originally designed for solopreneurs, but I've adapted it so it'll work great in a company of your size. In fact, we started putting the system in place during our values and mission conversation today. As we work with this system, you'll see how all the pieces fit together."

John recognizes the value of bringing in help. He hasn't felt this hopeful in years. "That's fine. I'm happy to bring in resources so Janice and Alicia can get up to speed. Even Stan. He's still operating in the dark ages. Maybe if we put together

a sales system, it'll bring us some positive results. We certainly have had a lousy run with trying to get new accounts. Seems that whenever we actually land a new account, and that's rare, we seem to lose one that's the very same size."

The waitress brings the food and sets it down before each of them. They pause and dig into their lunch.

John likes the feeling that the growth of the company is not all on him. The thought of Janice and Alicia, even Stan, working on a system to bring in new sales makes him want to sing.

Aaron realizes that they haven't talked about a major piece that needs to be put in place at Aardvark. It's important to have a sales and marketing system in place, yes, but they'll need to measure the right things so the management team and John will know if the company is moving in the right direction or not. They need to be able to track key numbers that they're currently ignoring. Revenue is one thing, but there are far more vital indicators of financial viability. And that's what John will need if he ever hopes to retire.

Aaron interrupts everyone's thoughts. "Janice, I'm assuming that you know what KPIs are."

"Of course," Janice says. "We always used them at my old company."

Aaron addresses John. "I'm assuming that you might not know what KPI means. It means key performance indicators. These are the numbers that drive a company, and not necessarily those found on your profit and loss statement of balance sheet. This is a hard exercise. Many companies have a hard time figuring out what moves the needle in the company. But, once you do, your work here will become more tightly focused."

Aaron now turns to Janice. "We need to put KPIs in place. I would like you to work on that before I come back again. Without a great scorecard, which our KPIs will provide to John, we won't know what's going on. And if John is flying

blind like that, there's little chance he'll actually let you run day-to-day operations the way you'd like to. Without knowledge about where you as a company stand, I can't see John staying out of your way."

No doubt skeptical that John will change his stripes, Janice frowns.

John feels hopeful. There may be enough structure to make him happy. He doesn't like the loose way the company has been running. This seems like a way to retain a sense of control.

"That sounds like a good idea," Janice says after a pause. "And I think it's something we need to do. I do like metrics. I like to know if we're on track. Now to see if John will trust me to do the job."

CHAPTER 16: IDENTIFYING THE BEST CUSTOMER

"The magic word," Aaron says, "is **no**. If you don't learn to say no, you don't have the capacity to say yes to the right customers. That means you need to help our sales department now by doing one thing: When it comes to marketing, you want to make sure you've identified who the right customer is. That means your message must be very clear."

Alicia seems confused. "What must it be clear about? That we only cater to certain customers?"

Aaron laughs. "Your values and mission must be integrated into your sales message." Aaron looks around the table where the management team is seated. "What's your mission statement?"

Alicia responds. "'We make our customers' lives easier.'"

"Yes, that's right. That's your mission. Can you do that? Can you make everybody's lives easier?"

Several nos waft through the room. John starts to squirm in his chair. He's never turned down business and still is having a hard time getting his arms around this concept. He and Aaron have talked about it, but he hasn't embraced the idea, at least not yet.

"Who can you make life easier for?"

Janice answers first. "People who need to have high-level foundry work done with complex finishing processes." She folds her arms across her chest.

"What else do you have to do?"

Now Janice looks confused. After a moment, however, she raises a finger in the air. "We have to be dealing with somebody who wants a small run, because we're not set up to do large runs."

Aaron is pleased. He knows Janice is a quick study. He's even more confident that he and John have placed her in the right role. "Okay. What else are you looking for?"

"We're probably not going to be selling to companies that have $1 billion in sales. We're probably going to sell to companies that are eight or nine times our size, but that's about it." Janice sits taller in her chair.

John stops squirming. He's starting to see how narrowing who the right customer is for Aardvark, and selling to them, might make operations simpler.

Aaron continues, "Okay. How often do your salespeople make calls or try to make calls on companies that have $1 billion in sales?"

This time Alicia answers. "A fair amount." She says this like she's just made a huge discovery about what isn't working at Aardvark.

"Are those the right people to call on?"

"No." It's Janice answering again.

"I suspected as much. Which is why I'm going to introduce you to a Michael Port theory. You're going to hear a lot of these today. The one we're going to talk about now is called the Red Velvet Rope Policy. Have you ever been out to a nightclub with a red velvet rope in front?" Aaron brings his fingertips together then stretches his arms wide. "What do you think it's there for?"

"To keep people out," Alicia says.

"What type of person are they keeping out?"

"They might be trying to keep out the wrong type of person, the riff-raff." She looks around and laughs. She's the youngest of the group, probably the only one who's been to a nightclub within the last decade, Aaron thinks.

"Right. And whether you think that's a good thing or a bad thing, they have a pretty good idea of who their best

customers are. As a result, they want only the right people getting past that red velvet rope.

"Now, I ask you, do you have a Red Velvet Rope Policy here at Aardvark Manufacturing?"

"Nope," Janice says. "We'll take anything that walks in the door." She all but groans.

"But, don't we have to take anything that walks in the door?" Alicia asks. "We're in business to sell. When times are tough, we can't afford to be choosy."

"Janice," Aaron says, ignoring Alicia's question for the moment, "what's one of the problems you have here?"

"For sure, one of the problems we have is that we don't make enough money."

Aaron raises one eyebrow. "And why don't you make enough money?"

"Could it be that we take on some business that we shouldn't?" Aaron has no doubt that Janice knows the answer and is playing along. She's too smart for that.

"That might be part of it. In fact, I would bet it is."

John pipes up, "You know that's part of it."

Aaron gives John a dirty look and admonishes him. "John, you're an observer, not a participant."

"Okay. Got it. I'll be quiet."

John looks around the table and makes eye contact with Aaron. He looks like he's going to explode, not because he's mad, but because he's used to inserting his opinion in every conversation. He's just starting to see how being quiet and sitting on the sidelines is good for him, and at the same time he's having a hard time doing it.

"You make your customers' lives easier," Aaron says. "So, you need to know and be very specific about what type of customer it is whose life you make easier." He opens his palms and presents them to Alicia. "Here's your first homework assignment and you're going to get a lot of them today.

You need to identify what your Red Velvet Rope Policy is here at Aardvark."

"How do I go about doing that?" she says.

"You need to start with a definition of your ideal customer, the person you serve best. We'll call this a persona. There are a couple of parts to a persona. The first part relates to the demographic—the size of the company, how much business it does, what kind of custom work they need done, and how it fits with the type of work you want to take on.

"The second part addresses the psychographic, including the type of company personality you're most successful with. You might notice that sometimes your very best and most profitable customers are those who have a certain type of personality. They might have a worldview that involves partnering with companies like yours, or they might be companies that only want to have their suppliers do what they tell them to do, nothing more. I think the truth is you're looking for customers who want a partner in developing their products. Your engineering skills are certainly a selling point in the world of companies that need small runs.

"I mean, there are some companies that would probably be a good fit, at least from a demographic point of view. They're the right size. They need the right product. You could even come up with a great solution for them except for the fact that they're very difficult to do business with. And, there's just no way to make money with a company that's difficult to do business with. You're just better off passing on that type of customer."

Janice sighs. No doubt, she knows precisely the type of customer Aaron is going on about. She's been the one responsible for answering all of the complaints.

"Here's my definition of a great customer: It's one that brings you above-average profits and below-average problems. When you combine these two things, you have happy people in-house, you have happy customers willing to talk

about you in a positive manner, and what you do is fun. That's what I want you folks to create. Your job is to help Stan find more of these types of customers."

"Regardless, what do we do with the customers we have now?" Alicia says. "A lot of them wouldn't make it past the red velvet rope, I can tell you that. What are we supposed to do? Fire them?"

Aaron smiles. He loves it when someone leads him into his next thought. "That's a good point. Thanks for bringing that up, Alicia. You need to consider this customer identification and selection as a process. You're going to do this over a period of time. You can't change who you service overnight. You're going to replace customers as you can, as you grow the business. You're going to find that, as you change your customer base to the 'right' customers, your profits will grow as well."

Fred pipes up. "That'll make my life a lot easier. I'm sick of juggling cash, and I bet John is, too."

John leans forward and starts to open his mouth but thinks better of it when Aaron shakes his finger at him.

"Here we go," Aaron says. "You know what your mission is: 'We make our customers' lives easier.' You know that by serving this mission, you will more than meet your financial goals. But what about values? Where do those fit in?"

"What are our values?" Alicia says. She'd been in all of the meetings, Aaron knows, but it isn't easy to keep all of the new concepts together in one's head. He gets that.

"Personal responsibility, financial security, innovation, rights and respect, and organizational mission," Aaron says.

"If we find customers who allow us to do all these things, then we've found our perfect customers?" Alicia says. From the look on her face, Aaron can see that she's having trouble connecting all of the pieces.

"That's absolutely correct," he says. "As you're thinking about building a Red Velvet Rope Policy, you first have to

think about how you integrate your values and your mission. The second step you need to take is to identify your target market and determine your niche."

"Wait," Janice says, raising her hand. "How do our values influence our Red Velvet Rope Policy? I understand how the mission influences this, but not our values. What do they have to do with target market and niche? You need to back up."

Aaron sees he's not done a good job tying mission to values. He tries again. "The truth is mission should always be a result of the values you bring to a company. The mission is a simple statement that allows you to use the company's core values in a positive manner. I know this is confusing. It will likely remain that way until you start talking about mission and values in the same sentence as much as possible."

Aaron wants to make clear the difference between market segment and niche, "I know you're wondering if these two things—target market and niche— are one and the same. They're not. Your target market is the industry and the people you want to do business with. Your niche, on the other hand, is the customers who would most likely appreciate the customized work that you do. Niche is always a subset of your target market. For example, your target market is the aircraft industry. But not all of them are ideal customers for you. Just the ones that want small runs and value high-end engineering work are. So, that would be your niche."

Janice says, "Who would be a great target market for us at Aardvark?"

"Aaron pauses and says, "They're businesses that:

- Do between $25 and maybe $100 million in sales;
- Need the sort of custom foundry work you do;
- Need something made from unusual metals;
- Need a high level of finishing and high quality; and
- Are willing to pay a little bit extra for it.

"Now, what niche do you serve?" Aaron continues. "Right now the answer to this question is all. That's part of the problem."

"But wouldn't a good niche be industries that we've learned a lot about and understand?" Alicia says.

"That probably would be true."

"One niche we've really been successful with and are really good at servicing is the aircraft industry." Alicia says this with some pride.

"That makes sense," Aaron says, "because you can do low-volume stuff with very high quality, and castings that they can't do in-house. This means one of your niches is high-quality foundry casting and finishing work for aircraft parts suppliers."

"That would be a good thing for us," Janice says. "We wouldn't have any problem servicing that."

Aaron says, "How many companies out there do you think service the aircraft industry and sell them parts? Meaning, how many of these companies could Aardvark be a supplier for?"

"I don't know. A couple hundred, probably," Janice says.

"With two salespeople, how long do you think it would take to contact a couple hundred folks and start proper conversations with them?"

"That could take six months to a year, I guess," Alicia says.

"That might keep you busy for a while. You're probably going to need to identify one or two other industries you can niche around. But you'll start off with the aircraft industry today."

" We now have a niche. Now, let's work on the next step."

"Building out this Red Velvet Rope Policy, this perfect customer profile, this niche identification, let's look at a concept that may be a little more challenging," Aaron says. "And

that's the recurring revenue model." He looks at Alicia and asks her, "What do we mean by a recurring revenue model?" She's been to business school, he thinks, she ought to know this.

"I'm not sure," Alicia says. "I'm not really sure I've ever even heard of that before."

"It's the secret to making a great business. Janice, what would you think a recurring revenue model is?"

"That's where people buy from you and you don't have to make a new sale every time, isn't it?"

"Yup. That's absolutely correct. At Aardvark, you tend to do one-offs, don't you? Which means you do really small runs that are individually designed and you only do them once. This process costs you tons of money and I'm not sure that you actually make money doing it."

"It's not easy to turn that kind of job down." Stan says, suddenly alert at the table. "You never know where a project like that could go. Anyway, that's what we're known for. That kind of work is our bread and butter. That's what I sell."

"You should think about only doing a one-off if there's a good possibility of leading to a contractual relationship where you produce the part over and over again," Aaron says. "So, you'll need a process to track and determine if you're doing too many one-offs. By one-off, I mean where you make the part once and never do it again. That's a lousy way to create a company that's sustainable. Aardvark really needs to have customers that are long term and need the same part done on a semi-regular basis, not just runs done once."

"We tend to do that," Janice says. "We always tend to be selling, so we don't get a lot of reorders. Correct?"

"Yes," Aaron says. "What if you could find companies who depended on you for a part and were actually subcontracting those parts to you, and they reorder it on a regular basis so you know at the beginning of the year approximate-

ly how much they're going to buy? What if you dealt with customers that work with you so closely they include you in their forecasting process?"

Alicia and Janice look at Aaron as if a light bulb is going on in each of their heads. Even Fred smiles. "I would love to have the ability to forecast in a predictable manner. It's been a frustration of mine for years."

"Wow," Alicia says. "If we did that, it would simplify so many other things around here. It would just make life a whole lot easier."

"You need to add that to your profile of a perfect customer," Aaron says. "Someone who's going to be a recurring revenue, repeat buyer—someone who's going to work with you on a regular basis without having to be sold anew every single time."

"Sounds good to us."

"Okay, then. You now have the beginnings of a marketing system. I'm hoping that you all are starting to get the idea that systems really are the stairway to heaven and something you badly need at Aardvark. Now that you know who the right customers are, you need to know how you can find them and what you can do to get Aardvark on their radar screen. Does your website describe any of that?"

"No," Alicia says. She laughs and shakes her head. "After what you just said, clearly our website is designed to attract everyone and their brother. I think we'll need to change it so it's talking to those in the aircraft parts business. That way, they'll know we understand their business and we can talk about how we make their life easier."

"Do you think you might want to make those changes?" Aaron asks the group.

"That sounds like a good idea. I think we need to get our website in place and saying the right things," says Stan. "It will make my job easier by far."

Aaron thinks for a minute, then addresses Stan. "Do you have companies that have been identified as potential clients?"

"We have a list."

"How many companies are on it?"

"About 150."

"Okay. How often do you communicate with them?"

Stan blinks. "That's a lot of people. I can't be getting to each and every one of them every month and still take care of our current customers."

"Anybody else?" Aaron asks.

"We don't really communicate with them," Janice says. She bites her lip.

"You don't have a newsletter then?"

This time it's Alicia who shakes her head.

"Don't you think you should?"

"We only have 150 companies," Alicia says.

"And what did you just say to me? That you're not communicating with them."

"Okay, maybe we should communicate with them." Alicia makes a note on her pad.

"If you communicate with them with a newsletter and follow it up every once in a while, do you think your sales department might have an easier time getting somebody to pick up the phone? Remember, marketing is about creating awareness of who you are and what you do.

"And you want to systematize your marketing efforts. A regularly scheduled newsletter will help you create that type of awareness. Regular communication will allow people to recognize that you can help solve their problems. And when you call, they'll pick up the phone.

"Remember, you need to find three things about your company that are unique and regularly communicate them.

This will really help you with your marketing message to the aircraft industry. When you have one thing that's unique, you sound like everyone else in your industry. When you have two things, you start to sound different. Three things usually helps you to stand out in a way none of your competitors do."

Alicia and Janice start writing down all the things they think they can do to help drive the effort. Aaron looks at it. "You have a pretty good list here," he says. "Let me ask you a question. How much extra time do you guys have to work on this stuff?"

"What extra time?" Alicia says.

"That's what I thought. You need to make sure you choose one thing at a time, get it done, and go on to the next thing. Remember, you want to borrow Gino Wickman's favorite saying, 'Less is more.'"

Aaron moves back to the head of the table and takes a sip of cold coffee. "Now, we need to talk about the sales process itself. There are two things about selling that I want you to know about, two terms I like a lot. One is a funnel and the other is a pipeline.

"Funnel," Alicia says. "I didn't know I'd be pouring liquid in this job. I thought that was what we did in the foundry."

Aaron likes that Alicia is lightening up. "In a way, that is actually what you'll be doing. What you want is a system by which you are able to attract the names of the right people to do business with. And as those people go through your funnel, they'll learn to gain more and more trust with you. For example, if you develop an e-book about how your innovation process involves collaboration, how Aardvark works with a customer's engineering team to create satisfying outcomes, would that be a start?"

"What do you mean?" Alicia says. "We're not writers. We make castings."

"Well, potential customers will visit your website. If you design your site correctly, potential customers might put in their email address and download the e-book about how they can outsource their need for high tolerance titanium parts. The e-book will help your potential customers know that you are specialists and Aardvark understands how to solve the problems your customers face.

"There are lots of things you can do to slowly build trust and allow a potential customer to know you for what you do. You want to make it easy for people know you're the right type of company to do business with. Having an e-book they can download or a regular blog post or even a video would allow potential customers to check you out and see if you're the type of company they might want to do business with. It's pretty simple, a funnel is the process where somebody you don't know finds you and you help them follow the road to become a prospect for Aardvark."

"Okay, that makes sense," Janice says. "What's this pipeline stuff?"

"A pipeline works like this: Once you qualify people as prospective customers, you actually put them into a sales process. You take steps to convert a prospect into a customer. Once somebody goes into your pipeline, they're assigned to a salesperson, they're assigned to a process, and you use a repeatable process that you can do over and over and over again—a process you know has a high probability of creating a customer.

"Can anyone tell me how you'd go about creating a pipeline?"

Alicia shrugs. "I don't have any idea."

Aaron looks at Janice. "How would you create a pipeline?"

"I'd probably do it like everything else I do in manufacturing," she says. "I would create a system."

Aaron smiles. If anyone wholly embraces the system mentality, it's Janice. She's the most savvy. "Okay, what would this system have, Janice?"

"We would start with an email or a letter. Then we would want to have a phone call where we set up an appointment. Next, we would visit with them to find out if we can help them, and then we would try to get them into our facility for a tour and a meeting with our engineering staff."

Aaron is impressed. He thinks this is a pretty good start to what a sales pipeline might look like. He also thinks that Aardvark will likely need a few more steps so he suggests, "You will want to think about all of the steps that it takes to create a customer and those steps should go into your pipeline process. This is a fantastic start on putting together a pipeline that will create new business for you. Not just any kind of business, but the kind of business that will allow you to make your customers happy and grow your profits.

"Remember, and this is important, both the pipeline and the funnel will be experiments. You never want to change everything at once. You'll try one thing, see how it works, and if it does what you want, you keep it. If it doesn't, then you want to let it go. Here's our mantra, 'Fail fast; fail cheap.'"

CHAPTER 17: **ALIGNMENT ACROSS THE BOARD**

"John, do you remember the first time we got together and had a conversation?" Aaron says.

"Yeah."

"Do you remember what I called it?"

"You called it the alignment something—the Alignment Conversation. Right?"

"Yes. Again, I have to thank my buddy, Mr. Port, for this. When I'm teaching the alignment process to somebody else, I call it the Super Simple Selling Process."

"Huh?" John is not the only one at the table that looks confused.

"During our Alignment Conversation, what happened?"

"I talked to myself about having to hire you. I was amazed I did, because I don't like consultants. I certainly didn't want to hire you. But I ended up doing it anyhow."

"Why did you do that, John?"

"I don't know." John puts his finger on his chin and thinks for a bit. *Why did I hire Aaron? That's a great question.* "We talked about stuff that was going on here and what I wanted to see happen and how there was this huge difference between the two and how unhappy I was. Then, you asked me what the value would be if I had things the way I wanted them." John pauses. "Ah," he says, "I see what you did."

"Right. You can sit back now." Aaron turns his attention to the rest of the group. They've been patient, but the day has been long. "We're now going to talk about the alignment process, which we're going to call our Super Simple Selling Process. I've established this process in multiple industries. It's been effective everywhere. Let me tell you how it works."

Aaron turns to address Stan. "Stan, I'm going to focus on you. That way, I can help you figure out whether someone who's come through the funnel needs to be put on the prospect list or not. This process has seven steps.

"Step 1: 'Where are you now?' is the first question you need to ask your prospect. In other words, what is the situation your potential customer has today? Are they having problems getting the parts built for them that they need? You'll also want to make sure that you focus the conversation on the types of parts they need because specifics matter.

"Step 2: 'Where would you like to be in the future?' is the second question you need to ask. The future, by the way, can be six months from now, one year, or even three years ahead. Make sure there's enough of a time gap to allow for you to help them make the changes they need in the time frame they have.

"Step 3: 'What is the difference between the two situations?' is the third question to explore. Here, you want to see if there is a big enough gap for your sales team to develop a program. If you've done a good job prospecting, you'll find that most of the time the answer is yes. If there's no real disparity between their current situation and what they want for the future, there's not much for you to work with.

"Step 4: 'What is the value of bridging the gap?' is the next question. If there is little or no value you can add, you need to end the conversation and move on. If the potential customer perceives lots of value, you'll ask, 'Would you like help solving this problem?' If the answer is yes, then you ask, 'Would you like to have us help you solve this problem?'

"Step 5: You've now uncovered a challenge that you can help this customer solve. You've determined the fact that there's an economic reason to solve this particular problem. You've quantified the economic return if you can help your potential customer solve the problem. The customer has acknowledged that they would like you to help them solve their problem. Now it's time to talk a little bit about who you are

and what you've done with other people to help them solve the same exact problem.

"Notice, you never talk about yourself until you know you can help in an economically positive manner, and the potential customer has said they want to work with you. This is where traditional sales people get in trouble. You don't want to waste your time talking about all of your capabilities until you know which capabilities to talk about.

"Step 6: You define the working relationship you are about to embark on with your potential customer as a collaborative process.

"Now, why do you talk about a collaborative process?"

"I know," Janice says. "That's pretty obvious to me."

"Not to me," Alicia says. "Maybe you could help me here."

Janice continues. "The best projects we work on are those where the client's engineers, our engineers, and our operations people all work together to solve a problem and come up with a solution that fits the client's needs. I would call that a collaborative process."

"That's exactly it," Aaron says. "Any successful client relationship is actually a collaboration. We don't think of it that way, but it really is. It's collaboration between the supplier and the buyer.

"Now, Aaron says, "The last step in this process is what I call the Rules Of The Road. We all have them, rules customers must follow if they are to work with us, or at least we should. My guess is your prospects have rules for their potential customers as well. You need to find out what their rules are, and your prospect needs to understand your rules. If they're compatible, these two sets of rules, then you move into the next stage." Aaron pauses. He realizes he's missed something important. "I have a question for you. If you asked this customer to buy at this point, do you think they would say yes?"

Stan opens his mouth to answer, then seemingly thinks better of it.

"I wouldn't," Janice says.

"I don't know," Alicia says. "It doesn't seem that we've spent enough time with this potential customer."

"I wouldn't buy, either," John says. Then, seeing Aaron staring at him, he stops.

"So," Aaron says. "You can only do so much with any customer based on the amount of trust you've earned. If you're going to build trust with a prospective customer, what would your next step be?"

"The best thing to do would be to have a conversation with their engineers and our engineers," Janice says.

"That would be one thing," Aaron says. "That might be part of your pipeline. Or could it be that you want to have them come out here and kick the tires? That would be a good thing, too. That should be something we put on the list also."

Janice picks up her pencil again and makes more notes.

"You need to identify the steps that you take people through logically. And they need to be in line with the amount of trust you've earned thus far. When you do that, you now have a marketing-and-sales system that's not just rational and makes sense, but also repeatable. You can't invite them in for a day-long tour if you've only had a 15-minute conversation over the phone. Are you willing to work on that between now and the next meeting?"

Alicia and Janice both agree.

"Now," Aaron says, "make sure as you go through this process that we talk about what you're developing, because I'm not going to be out here again for a few months. That's going to give you guys plenty of time to get started on this. Remember, one step at a time, get it done, and then move on."

Janice and Alicia look nervous. They'll be the ones in charge of implementing most of the changes. Stan looks more curious than anything.

"What do you think you might want to work on first? Do you want to work on your marketing system, or do you want to work on your sales system?"

Alicia looks at Janice. "I don't know, Janice. What do you think?"

Janice pauses and says, "We could work on the marketing system, but that's not going to solve our immediate problem, is it?"

John looks at them in silence and shakes his head.

"I kind of like the marketing thing more," Alicia says.

"That doesn't solve our problem," Janice says.

"But I want to do marketing." Alicia's tone betrays some annoyance.

"Alicia," Janice says, "we need to fix what's broken here first, and our sales system is broken. I'm going to say, and I get the final vote on this, we work on sales first." She looks at Aaron and says, "What do you think?"

"I think that makes sense. While I'm gone, I want both of you to make sure we set up several calls to put together a sales system that will help you have high quality conversations with potential customers so you know whether you're doing the right things or you're just spinning your wheels."

With that, Aaron looks at John and says, "I think I've done about as much damage as your company can handle right now. Why don't we call it a day? John, let's plan to spend about 90 minutes tomorrow morning doing a recap of where we are, and then you can give me a ride to the airport."

CHAPTER 18: **TYING UP LOOSE ENDS**

It's 10 p.m. and John thinks about what's happened over the past six months. He's starting to feel some hope. John has gone from really hating his job and his relationship with his family to being in a place where he can see some light at the end of the tunnel. Working with Aaron has been challenging and at times he wanted to pull the plug. Looking back, he's glad he didn't. His company isn't fixed by a long shot, but he sees a way forward, one that will help with all the issues that he had when he first talked with his attorney at the mixer, which seems like a million years ago now. He knows there's work to be done and sees a lot more positive than negative. He's ready for the next stage and knows that making some small changes can have a big effect in his business and his life.

Before he goes to sleep, he turns to Anne, "You know the work that I've done with Aaron is starting to pay off. I'm pretty sure that we're actually going to be able to get away for two weeks and my goal is going to be to not call the office once."

Anne smiles. "That would be really wonderful, John. At first, I wasn't thrilled about another consultant, but it looks like this one actually got your attention. I'm not sure how it happened, but that doesn't matter as long as it did."

John smiles to himself and drifts off to sleep looking forward to his meeting with Aaron the next day.

The next morning, Aaron and John once again get together in John's office for a recap of the past several weeks. Aaron feels there has been some progress and reason to feel at least a little optimistic. John feels and looks like he's been taken through a wringer and, in many respects, he has.

Each man sits lost in his thoughts.

Although John is tired, he feels that for the first time in years there might be a future he could be happy with. He knows that he is lucky to have attracted Janice to the company. He thinks she is going to do a really good job running the day-to-day operations of the company. He also knows that he has to remember that when Janice makes mistakes he needs to have some tolerance and make sure there is a learning opportunity along the way. He knows that he is going to have to show some patience and at the same time keep pushing for changes that have to be made.

He also has some hope that he and his wife will finally be able to get away for some extended time together. It feels good that he's able to tell her that he thinks they'll finally be able to get away sometime in the next year. He hopes that he'll be able to rekindle his relationship with her and that they can just have some fun together like they did when they first got married.

John also feels pretty good about his daughter, Alicia. He feels that their session yesterday afternoon was a good one. The only dark spot he sees is his son, Adam. He has serious doubts about whether Adam will be able to stay in the company. At the same time, he doesn't dare let anyone know what he's thinking, especially Aaron.

Aaron has also been thinking about the past several weeks. He's been down this road many times before. Most of the time, he comes away from the first part of his work with companies feeling pretty good about the progress that has been made. This is the way he's feeling about his time with John and Aardvark.

He suspects that John is still worried about his son, Adam. He also suspects that both John and Adam feel that it's different this time around. He thinks John feels bad for his son and that Adam is probably more than a little scared about what his future holds.

Aaron is glad that Janice is in the mix. Having Janice at the company is a fortunate occurrence. Usually, there would be no one internally who could take the role of operations manager and relieve the owner enough for operational irrelevance to occur. Aaron feels that, in this case, Janice will be more than adequate in the role of COO, which will allow John to become operationally irrelevant.

He's happy that, during the first part of the engagement, John was able to make some real progress in moving the company forward in understanding and in making plans to address all five areas of business sustainability. Now, the hard part is about to start. Aaron knows that implementation is where the rubber meets the road. Talk is one thing, but action is what counts.

Aaron turns toward John and starts the day's conversation, "John, we only have a couple of hours left before I have to leave. Why don't we review where we stand and what two or three things you want to accomplish before I come back again."

John realizes that he's been deep in thought and snaps out of his head. He looks at Aaron. "That would be a good idea."

Aaron thinks for a second and starts. "Let's do a review of the five areas of sustainability and see where we stand on each. I want you to know that, in my opinion, your company has made some great progress. But, it's only a beginning and the real work starts now."

John just nods.

Aaron dives in. "Let's start with what I think is the most important part of the work you have immediately in front of you."

"And what might that be?"

"I think the first thing I want you to commit to is working on becoming operationally irrelevant. That means you're going to have to develop a strong working relationship with Janice and you're going to have to let her do the job.

"There are some things Janice will have no problem with. That would include manufacturing and quality control. She's going to have quite a learning curve with marketing and sales, as well as finance. I'll be talking with Janice on a regular basis about both areas, helping her to learn what she needs to know.

"The challenge you're going to face is learning to send problems to Janice and to not lose your cool when mistakes happen. Because Janice has little experience with finance or sales, you can be sure she'll make mistakes. When those mistakes happen, what are you going to do?"

John rubs his chin. "I guess I'm going to help Janice learn what the mistake is and then help her learn from it."

"And, what specifically are you going to ask Janice when one of those dreaded mistakes happens?"

John has to think for a few seconds before answering. "I'm going to ask her what she learned."

"What if Janice doesn't know the answer? What are you going to do then?"

"If I know the answer myself, I'll have Janice make some guesses and help her figure out what needs to be done. If I don't know the answer, I'll help her think through where she can find what she needs to do. If I do my job properly, I'm going to tell her to call you a lot."

"That's great, John. I want you to make sure that you use me as a resource even when I'm not here. Most of the things that Janice will need help with are things that will only take 10 or 20 minutes of her time."

Aaron feels confident that John understands the basics of becoming operationally irrelevant, but there is one more thing he wants to hammer home.

"John, what we've been talking about for the past few minutes is you becoming operationally irrelevant. And there's one major piece that we need to talk about regarding that."

"What's that?"

"Remember when we talked about EIA: expect, inspect, accept?"

"Of course."

"John, you're going to try to stay out of operations and let Janice run the company. You'll be doing a lot of delegating while doing this. Delegating that you've never done before. Do you remember our conversation about the biggest mistake you're likely to make around delegation?"

John thinks for a minute and remembers. "I want to make sure I delegate and not abdicate. For me to do that I need to remember to inspect and not just set an expectation. And when I inspect, there's a good chance I'll be finding mistakes and we already talked about what I need to do when I see mistakes being made."

Aaron flashes a big smile. "You've got it. Let's move on to the second thing I want you to focus on. Let's talk about what you're going to do as it relates to your values and mission here. This is where you're going to need to stay involved. In fact, you're the holder of both. If you don't pay lots of attention to both, then it's going to be hard for everyone to stay focused on what needs to be done.

"John, do you remember what our five values are and how they're going to be used?"

John knows the values but he's still unclear on how they'll be used. "I think we need to have a fast review. Let me first list the values and see if I have them right:

"Personal responsibility, where we are accountable for our own actions and the results of those actions.

"Financial security, where the company makes enough money to provide an adequate return for the business as well as for those who work in the business.

"Innovation, where we provide our customers with products that makes their business better.

"Rights and respect, where we respect each other as human beings.

"Organizational mission, where we focus on the five areas of sustainability to create a great business for all of our stakeholders."

Aaron is impressed. "John, you really have that nailed. Now tell me, how are you going to use these values on a daily basis?"

John frowns. "That's where I'm stuck. I'm not really sure how I use them. I know you want to ask a bunch of questions around this but we're almost out of time. Can you, just this time, tell me the answer?"

Aaron laughs. "Sure, but it's just this time. There are three ways you're going to use these values.

"First, you're going to use them to craft a mission statement that all your stakeholders understand and can follow.

"Then, you'll use the values to coach the people you work with when their behavior is out of alignment with them.

"Finally, you'll use them when you communicate with your stakeholders about what's important and different about your company. Not everyone will resonate with them and that's okay. You want the right people to resonate with them and those are the people and companies you and the team at Aardvark are meant to serve.

"Now, can you tell me what your mission statement is and how it fits in with your values?"

John pauses and thinks for a little while before responding. "'We make our customers' lives easier.'"

Aaron wants something more from John. "Now I want you to tie your mission statement and values together."

John is confused. He gets how the mission is important, but he hasn't thought about how the company values and mission tie together. He stops talking, stares out the window and thinks. About two minutes later, he's ready with his answer.

"To make our customers' lives better, we start by developing better solutions to their problems. That comes from innovation. Showing personal responsibility means we don't give our customers excuses when we make mistakes. We own our mistakes and solve them quickly.

"We demand that all our employees show respect toward our customers and don't allow any badmouthing toward a customer or allow poor communications from our customers toward our employees. We also price our products fairly so our customers can get a good return and we're making the amount of money we need to be sustainable.

"Finally, when we pay attention to what makes a company sustainable, it makes it easier for our customers to do business with us and for them to get an outstanding result from the work we do for them."

Again, Aaron is impressed. He didn't think John would be able to tie all his values together.

"John, it looks to me like you've really been thinking about values and mission. I love the way you've tied all of them into what your mission means. Now, your job for the next six months is to find a way to talk about your mission as it relates to your values every day. Do you think you can do this?"

John gets a huge grin on his face and thinks back to where they started. He almost shouts, "You bet I can."

Aaron moves on to the next thing that Aardvark needs to focus on. This is getting their sales in order. Aardvark does too many one-off jobs and they need to develop customers that understand the company mission and values. He also knows the company needs to develop customers who reorder on a regular basis. This is as close as they can get to having a business with a recurring revenue model, the third stage of a sustainable company.

"John, the last thing I want you to really focus on before I come back is getting your marketing and sales program

turned around and doing the right things. First, you need to find a way for the right customers to find you and for you to find them. Then you need to develop a predictable sales model that will lead your potential customers to know that you're the right company for them and that you can solve their problems more easily than your competitors.

"You're going to find that although this looks simple, it's not. There are two things I'm worried about. First, Alicia is pretty green around this subject. She picks things up quickly but she'll have to spend a lot of time with me on the phone. This is especially important because Janice will be supervising her and Janice is not a sales pro either. I'm pretty sure we can get a sales system in place that predictably produces sales from the type of customers you want.

"Second, I'm worried about Stan. He's an old-time sales guy and I'm not sure he's going to be able to or want to work within a system. Let's give him all the help he needs and at the same time you'll have to be watching what he does to make sure he gets with your new program. If he doesn't, then you'll have a hard decision to make. Does that make sense?"

John thinks for a little while. He doesn't like the answer, but he says it anyway. "I get it. This is the sort of thing I'm not looking forward to at all. Stan has been with me for a really long time."

Aaron looks at his watch and realizes that time is getting short. He needs to head to the airport. "We don't have much time left and I want to review the last two parts before we leave. You're not going to do much about profits right now, but at the same time you are."

"I don't get it. What do you mean?"

"There's something very important you need to understand about profits. Profits are a result and, at the same time, there are actions you can take to improve your profits. Fixing your sales process is an example of fixing your profit problem. Getting recurring orders will help improve your profit

picture and being more systematic about how you run your business will also improve your profits. But, at the end of the day, profits are a result of the actions you take.

"You'll be focusing on what we talked about and your profits will get better. I don't think you'll see enough profits to take care of the four areas of profits you need, but I'm sure you'll be seeing improvements over the next six months.

"John, do you remember what the four areas of profits we need to cover are?"

"I sure do. Here they are:

"Enough profit for me to have a good lifestyle.

"Enough money in the bank for a six-month cushion as an emergency fund.

"Enough extra cash so we can afford to grow the business.

"Excess cash that will allow me to fund my retirement fund adequately."

Aaron takes a final look at his watch and sees he has about ten minutes left before he absolutely must leave.

"John, there's one final thing to creating a sustainable business and you have a great person for it.

"One of the things I really like about Janice is her big company experience. She's just the person to bring systems to your company. I know it's not your strong suit, but it is Janice's. You're going to have to let her run with the ball on this and you're going to have to back her up when people come to you and complain about the systems she'll be putting in place."

John nods in agreement.

Aaron has something he wants to say. "I want to tell you that our work together has been really satisfying for me. I think we've done some really good work and you've done a great job of taking your first steps in lots of different areas.

"I'm going to want to have a call with you every two weeks to monitor your progress. I'm also going to be setting

up regular calls with Janice and Alicia. I'll be back in three months to work through what you've accomplished and what's next on the list. Until then, I want you to not only look at what needs to be done, I also want you to look at what you've accomplished. Do you think you can do that?"

John nods again. He thinks about where he was three months ago and where he is now. He feels like it's different this time. He hopes it lasts and things keep getting better. He thinks that he needs to send his attorney a very nice bottle of wine. If Aaron hadn't shown up when he did, he'd be in a very different place.

John looks at Aaron. "First, thanks for the work you've done with me and my company. Second, you're a bit crusty and, in a way, curmudgeonly. But if you weren't, I don't think you would have gotten through to me. You're the right person for me and I'm looking forward to the future now. Something I couldn't have said three months ago.

"Let me walk you out to your car."

The two walk out through the lobby. Aaron gets in his car and waves. John watches as Aaron drives off. He thinks to himself that his business is starting to get to be fun again. He wonders where he'll be and what his life and business will be three years from now.

He feels good about the future and decides to surprise Anne and go home early. Clearly, it's time to celebrate with her.

RECOMMENDED **READING LIST**

This is a partial list of books I recommend for all business owners. Many of these are cited in the text of the book. If you have books you think should be added, just email me at *Jpatrick@stage2solution.com* and let me know what I missed.

These books are listed in alphabetical order. I have grouped them by subject.

MANAGEMENT

The Advantage: Why Organizational Health Trumps Everything Else in Business, Lencioni, Patrick, Jossey-Bass, 2012

Conscious Capitalism: Liberating the Heroic Spirit of Business, Mackey, John E., Rajendra S. Sisodia, Harvard Business Review Press, 2013

Drive: The Surprising Truth About What Motivates Us, Pink, Daniel H., Riverhead Books, 2009

The Effective Executive: The Definitive Guide to Getting the Right Things Done, Drucker, Peter F., HarperBusiness, 1966

The Essential Drucker: The Best of Sixty Years of Peter Drucker's Essential Writings on Management, Drucker, Peter F., Regan Books, 2000

First, Break All The Rules: What the World's Greatest Managers Do Differently, Buckingham, Marcus, Curt Coffman, Gallup Press, 1998

Great by Choice: Uncertainty, Chaos, and Luck—Why Some Thrive Despite Them All, Collins, James C., Morten T. Hansen, HarperBusiness, 2011

The Knack: How Street-Smart Entrepreneurs Learn to Handle Whatever Comes Up, Brodsky, Norm, Bo Burlingham, Portfolio Hardcover, 2008

Management: Tasks, Responsibilities, Practices, Drucker, Peter F., HarperBusiness, 1985

Profit First: A Simple System to Transform Any Business from a Cash-Eating Monster to a Money-Making Machine, Michalowicz, Mike, Obsidian Press, 2014

Rocket Fuel: The One Essential Combination That Will Get You More of What You Want from Your Business, Wickman, Gino, Mark C. Winters, BenBella Books, 2015

Scaling Up: How a Few Companies Make It...and Why the Rest Don't, Harnish, Verne, Gazelles Inc., 2014

Smarter Faster Better: The Secrets of Being Productive in Life and Business, Duhigg, Charles, Random House, 2016

The Speed of Trust: The One Thing that Changes Everything, Covey, Stephen M.R., Free Press, 2006

MARKETING

80/20 Sales and Marketing: The Definitive Guide to Working Less and Making More, Marshall, Perry, Richard Koch, Entrepreneur Press, 2013

Ask: The Counterintuitive Online Method to Discover Exactly What Your Customers Want to Buy...Create a Mass of Raving Fans...and Take Any Business to the Next Level, Levesque, Ryan, Dunham Books, 2015

Book Yourself Solid Illustrated: The Fastest, Easiest, and Most Reliable System for Getting More Clients Than You Can Handle Even If You Hate Marketing and Selling, Port, Michael, Wiley, 2006

Brainfluence: 100 Ways to Persuade and Convince Consumers with Neuromarketing, Dooley, Roger, John Wiley and Sons, 2011

Hug Your Haters: How to Embrace Complaints and Keep Your Customers, Baer, Jay, Portfolio, 2016

Perennial Seller: The Art of Making and Marketing Work that Lasts, Holiday, Ryan, Portfolio, 2017

Surge: Time the Marketplace, Ride the Wave of Consumer Demand, and Become Your Industry's Big Kahuna, Michalowicz, Mike, Obsidian Press, 2016

Unstoppable Referrals: 10x Referrals Half the Effort, Gordon, Steve, Unstoppable CEO Press, 2014

FAMILY BUSINESS

Business is Business: Reality Checks for Family-Owned Companies, Kolbe, Kathy, Amy Bruske, Greenleaf Book Group Press, 2017

The Defining Decade: Why Your Twenties Matter—And How to Make the Most of Them Now, Jay, Meg, Twelve, 2012

Intentional Wealth: How Families Build Legacies of Stewardship and Financial Health, Pullen, Courtney, Createspace, 2013

SALES

The Challenger Customer: Selling to the Hidden Influencer Who Can Multiply Your Results, Adamson, Brent, Matthew Dixon, Pet Spenner, Nick Toman, Portfolio, 2015

The Challenger Sale: Taking Control of the Customer Conversation, Dixon, Matthew, Brent Adamson, Portfolio, 2011

Launch: An Internet Millionaire's Secret Formula to Sell Almost Anything Online, Build a Business You Love, and Live the Life of Your Dreams, Walker, Jeff, Morgan James Publishing, 2014

The New Rules of Sales and Service: How to Use Agile Selling, Real-Time Customer Engagement, Big Data, Content, and Storytelling to Grow Your Business, Scott, David Meerman, John Wiley and Sons, 2014

Selling the Invisible: A Field Guide to Modern Marketing, Beckwith, Harry, Warner Books, 1997

Swim with the Sharks Without Being Eaten Alive: Outsell, Outmanage, Outmotivate, and Outnegotiate Your Competition, MacKay, Harvey, HarperBusiness, 1988

To Sell is Human: The Surprising Truth About Moving Others, Pink, Daniel H., Canongate Books, 2013

LEADERSHIP

Changing for Good: A Revolutionary Six-Stage Program for Overcoming Bad Habits and Moving Your Life Positively Forward, Prochaska, James O., John C. Norcross, Carlo C. DiClemente, William Morrow, 1994

Immunity to Change: How to Overcome It and Unlock the Potential in Yourself and Your Organization (Leadership for the Common Good), Kegan, Robert, Lisa Laskow Lahey, Harvard Business Review Press, 2009

Leaders Eat Last: Why Some Teams Pull Together and Others Don't, Sinck, Simon, Portfolio, 2013

The Leadership Challenge: How to Make Extraordinary Things Happen in Organizations, Kouzes, James M., Barry Z. Posner, Jossey-Bass, 1987

Principle-Centered Leadership, Covey, Stephen R., Fireside Press, 1991

Team of Teams: New Rules of Engagement for a Complex World, McChrystal, General Stanley, Tantum Collins, Portfolio, 2015

What Got You Here Won't Get You There: How Successful People Become Even More Successful, Goldsmith, Marshall, Mark Reiter, Hyperion, 2007

PEOPLE MANAGEMENT

Assholes: A Theory, James, Aaron, Anchor, 2012

Talent is Overrated: What Really Separates World-Class Performers from Everybody Else, Colvin, Geoff, Portfolio, 2008

Tribal Leadership: Leveraging Natural Groups to Build a Thriving Organization, Logan, Dave, John King, Halee Fischer-Wright, HarperBusiness, 2008

Triggers: Creating Behavior That Lasts—Becoming the Person You Want to Be, Goldsmith, Marshall, Mark Reiter, Crown Business, 2015

NEGOTIATING

Crucial Conversations: Tools for Talking When Stakes Are High, Patterson, Kerry, Joseph Grenny, Ron McMillan, Al Switzler, McGraw-Hill, 2001

Never Split the Difference: Negotiating As If Your Life Depended On It, Voss, Chris, Tahl Raz, HarperBusiness, 2016

INNOVATION

Competing Against Luck: The Story of Innovation and Customer Choice, Christensen, Clayton M., Taddy Hall, Karen Dillon, David S. Duncan, HarperBusiness, 2016

The Innovator's Solution: Creating and Sustaining Successful Growth, Christensen, Clayton M., Michael E. Raynor, Harvard Business School Press, 2003

BUSINESS SUCCESSION PLANNING

The Completely Revised How to Run Your Business So You Can Leave It in Style, Brown, John H., Kathryn B. Carroll, Business Enterprise Press, 1990

Sell Your Business for an Outrageous Price: An Insider's Guide to Getting More Than You Ever Thought Possible, Short, Kevin, AMACOM/American Management Association, 2014

LEAN MANUFACTURING

Out of the Crisis, Deming, W. Edwards, MIT Press, 1982

The Remedy: Bringing Lean Thinking Out of the Factory to Transform the Entire Organization, Dennis, Pascal, John Wiley and Sons, 2010

Scrum: The Art of Doing Twice the Work in Half the Time, Sutherland, Jeff, JJ Sutherland, Crown Business, 2014

The Toyota Way to Lean Leadership: Achieving and Sustaining Excellence Through Leadership Development, Liker, Jeffrey K., Gary L. Convis, McGraw Hill, 2011

MISCELLANEOUS

Better by Mistake: The Unexpected Benefits of Being Wrong, Tugend, Alina, Riverhead Books, 2011

Critical Path, Fuller, R. Buckminster, Kiyoshi Kuromiya, St. Martin's Griffin, 1981

Deep Work: Rules for Focused Success in a Distracted World, Newport, Cal, Grand Central Publishing, 2016

Experience Economy: Work Is Theatre & Every Business a Stage, Pine II, B. Joseph, James H. Gilmore, Harvard Business Review Press, 1999

Give and Take: Why Helping Others Drives Our Success, Grant, Adam, Viking, 2013

The Happiness Advantage: The Seven Principles That Fuel Success and Performance at Work, Achor, Shawn, Crown Business, 2010

Misbehaving: The Making of Behavioral Economics, Thaler, Richard H., W.W. Norton & Company, 2015

Predictably Irrational: The Hidden Forces That Shape Our Decisions, Ariely, Dan, HarperCollins Canada, 2008

Steal the Show: From Speeches to Job Interviews to Deal-Closing Pitches, How to Guarantee a Standing Ovation for All the Performances in Your Life, Port, Michael, Houghton Mifflin Harcourt, 2015

Think Like a Freak: The Authors of Freakonomics Offer to Retrain Your Brain, Levitt, Steven D., Stephen J. Dubner, William Morrow, 2014

Time Really Is Money: How To Make $5,000 Per Hour, Slee, Rob, Burn the Boat Press, 2015

The Undoing Project: A Friendship That Changed Our Minds, Lewis, Michael, W.W. Norton & Company, 2016

Virtual Freedom: How to Work with Virtual Staff to Buy More Time, Become More Productive, and Build Your Dream Business, Ducker, Chris, BenBella Books, 2014

BUSINESS FABLES

The Alchemist, Coelho, Paulo, HarperCollins, 1993

The Five Dysfunctions of a Team: A Leadership Fable, Lencioni, Patrick, Jossey-Bass, 2002

Get A Grip: How to Get Everything You Want from Your Entrepreneurial Business, Wickman, Gino, Mike Paton, BenBella Books, 2012

Getting Naked: A Business Fable About Shedding The Three Fears That Sabotage Client Loyalty, Lencioni, Patrick, Jossey-Bass, 2002

The Goal: A Process of Ongoing Improvement, Goldratt, Eliyahu M., Jeff Cox, North River Press, 1984

Greater Than Yourself: The Ultimate Lesson of True Leadership, Farber, Steve, Crown Business, 2009

The Ideal Team Player: How To Recognize and Cultivate the Three Essential Virtues, Lencioni, Patrick M., Jossey-Bass, 2016

The Radical Leap: A Personal Lesson in Extreme Leadership, Farber, Steve, Dearborn Trade, 2004

MEMOIRES AND BIOGRAPHIES

Creativity, Inc.: Overcoming the Unseen Forces That Stand in the Way of True Inspiration, Catmull, Ed, Amy Wallace, Random House, 2014

Delivering Happiness: A Path to Profits, Passions, and Purpose, Hsieh, Tony, Grand Central Publishing, 2010

Elon Musk: Tesla, SpaceX, and the Quest for a Fantastic Future, Vance, Ashlee, Ecco, 2015

In the Plex: How Google Thinks, Works, and Shapes Our Lives, Levy, Steven, Simon and Schuster, 2011

Onward: How Starbucks Fought for Its Life without Losing Its Soul, Schultz, Howard, Joanne Gordon, Rodale Books, 2011

The Pixar Touch: The Making of a Company, Price, David A., Knopf, 2008

Shoe Dog: A Memoir by the Creator of Nike, Knight, Phil, Scribner, 2016

The Virgin Way: Everything I Know About Leadership, Branson, Richard, Portfolio, 2014

COOL STUFF

CORE VALUES

If you're interested in taking your own core value analysis for your company, go to *www.sustainablethebook.com* and use access code *Aardvark* and do our down-and-dirty core value quiz where you get to rate your company on the 18 value drivers that are discussed in this book. The Sustainable business address is: *www.sustainablebusiness.co*.

ACKNOWLEDGEMENTS

It takes a village to create a book and bring it to life. That has certainly been true in my journey.

First, I want to thank my book coach, Ann Sheybani, for her gracious and consistent work on this book. If it wasn't for her, I'm sure this book would have never been completed and it certainly would not be as good as it is.

Then, of course, there are the many mentors I've had over the years, starting with my first mentors in the vending and food service business. A special mention goes to J. Shields Harvey who took me under his wing and helped prevent me flaming out and going bankrupt during my first three years in business.

In the financial services and consulting world, there are too many to mention. I've had both real and virtual mentors, including Rob Slee, Susan Bradley, John A. Warnick, Richard Wagner, Randy Fox, Scott Hamilton, Scott Fithian, Kathy Kolbe, John Brown, Michael Port, and Mike Michalowicz. To these people and to the hundreds that I'm sure I've left out, I want to say thanks for your help.

Finally, I want to thank my family: Suzanne, Sam and Alexa. They put up with me working long hours while I was learning and running my businesses, obsessing about it all, and missing family events. While this book is the culmination of forty years of study and experience, of the lessons I've learned and applied along the way, without my family's support, this journey would have been so much more difficult if not impossible.

ABOUT THE AUTHOR

Josh Patrick is a serial entrepreneur and advisor to private business owners. He has not only studied what it takes to create a sustainable business, but he's lived it as well. He now spends his time helping other private businesses do what it takes to become economically and personally sustainable in their business and life.

Josh lives in Hinesburg, Vermont with his wife, Suzanne, his dog, Oscar, and cat, Toby, (or, as Josh likes to call him, Napolean). When Josh is not obsessing about sustainability, he loves to read, ski, bike, and listen to great live music.

Made in the USA
Columbia, SC
19 January 2018